Aug 1993
May Henderson
Jean Schuster

THE
LAST DAYS
THE
MIDDLE EAST
AND ### THE
BOOK OF
REVELATION

THE
LAST DAYS
THE
MIDDLE EAST
AND
THE
BOOK OF
REVELATION

CHUCK SMITH WITH DAVID WIMBISH

Chosen Books

A Division of Baker Book House
Grand Rapids, Michigan 49516

Unless noted otherwise Scripture texts are from the Holy Bible, New International Version, copyright © 1973, 1978, 1984 International Bible Society. Used by permission of Zondervan Bible Publishers.

Library of Congress Cataloging-in-Publication Data

Smith, Chuck, 1927 June 25–
    The last days, the Middle East, and the book of Revelation / Chuck Smith with David Wimbish.
        p.   cm.
    Rev. ed. of : Dateline earth. c 1989.
    ISBN 0-8007-9185-1
    1. Bible. N.T. Revelation—Prophecies.   2. Iraq-Kuwait Crisis,
1990- —Prophecies. I. Wimbish, David. II. Smith, Chuck, 1927
June 25- Dateline earth.   III. Title.
BS2825.2.S65   1991
236′.9—dc20   91-11783
                                                                          CIP

A Chosen Book
Copyright © 1991 by Chuck Smith
Chosen Books are published by Fleming H. Revell
a division of Baker Book House Company
P.O. Box 6287, Grand Rapids, Michigan 49516-6287

Third printing, March 1993

Printed in the United States of America

To my devoted and faithful wife, Kay, a constant source of inspiration and blessing. To our four children, Jan, Chuck, Jeff, and Cheryl, whom we consider special gifts from God, and their God-chosen mates who have presented to us 15 grandchildren who are super special gifts. Also to all of you who through the grace of God will share with us the glories of His eternal Kingdom.

Contents

_p. 170_

THE LAST DAYS

THE MIDDLE EAST

AND THE BOOK OF REVELATION

1

Unveiling the Future

As I write these words, people the world over are anxiously tuned to the news stations on their radios and televisions.

Bombs and missiles are falling throughout the Middle East.

Innocent men, women and children are dying because of one man's greed and arrogance—one man who sees himself as a modern-day reincarnation of the ancient Babylonian king Nebuchadnezzar. Of course I am talking about Saddam Hussein, bloody ruler of Iraq, whose thirst for power has pushed the world to the very brink of the abyss.

Everywhere, people are asking the same questions: "Is this the beginning of the end?" "Could Saddam Hussein be the Antichrist?" "What are the events that will lead up to the final great battle at Armageddon?"

People who have not been to church in years are dusting off their Bibles and turning to the book of Revelation to see if it doesn't have something to say about what is going on in these most perilous times. From the dim recesses of their memories, they are recalling words such as *tribulation, Armageddon, the mark of the beast,* and trying to make sense out of them.

Recently, I heard a non-Christian ask the question. "Doesn't your Bible have something to say about all this?"

Indeed it does.

A few days ago, one of the major newspapers in our area carried a political cartoon regarding the current situation in the

Middle East. The cartoon depicted a religious "fanatic," complete with long hair and a flowing robe, holding a sign that read: *The end is near.* Standing nearby was a well-dressed businessman. But rather than deriding the "prophet," as is usually the case with onlookers, his comment was, "You know . . . I have a feeling you may be right this time."

That cartoon shows how pervasive the feeling is that the Last Days may very well be upon us. I believe, from an extensive study of Scripture, that they are.

Someday soon—I believe within my lifetime—a man is going to come along who will bring the entire world together under his leadership. This man will be hailed as the wisest, most efficient, most humane leader who ever lived.

But beneath it all, he will be a seething cauldron of hatred, and he will especially abhor those who have anything at all to do with God—even though he, himself, claims to be God's chosen leader.

He will be the Antichrist, and his appearance on the world stage is foretold by the book of Revelation (among other biblical books).

But Saddam Hussein is not that man.

How can I say that with such certainty? Because several things that have not yet happened must take place before the Antichrist rises to power. For one, the Soviet Union will launch an unsuccessful attack on Israel and, in the process, be relegated to the status of a second-rate power. The vacuum that is created by Russia's demise will help pave the way for the Antichrist's ascendancy in Western Europe.

Some people may see Iraq's attacks on Israel with Soviet-built Scud missiles as this foretold invasion of Israel, but the involvement of the U.S.S.R. will not be so hidden. When the invasion comes it will be a full-fledged attack; it will not be carried out by proxy. Russia itself will be very much involved.

There are other events that must happen before the Antichrist gets here, and we will talk more about them as we go along. But, again, it is most unlikely that he has as yet made his first public appearance. I suspect strongly that he is alive and well somewhere right now—biding his time.

It is easy to see someone like Saddam Hussein as the Antichrist because he is so openly evil and so openly hostile to American interests. But the Antichrist is more likely to arise from a power that has long been the friend of the United States. To those who are not discerning, he will seem to be a friend.

At the same time, Hussein is certainly doing a good job of preparing the way for him—testing the technologies that he will use to subjugate the world and fanning Arab mistrust and hatred of the Jews, for starters. His insistence that his kingdom is a modern-day version of ancient Babylon only adds to the demonic flavor of his character.

After all, the book of Revelation has much to say about Babylon, and none of it is good. To put it simply, God and Babylon (in any form) do not get along. They never have; they never will. And that is very bad news for the Babylonians among us.

Who, then, is Saddam Hussein? Simply one of the many players in Satan's grand design to wrest this universe away from God's control. He is not *the* central human character in this drama, but he is a pretty fair stand-in until the central character comes along.

This most recent war in the Middle East is not the final battle, but we might consider it to be a dress rehearsal. Before too many months have gone by, the entire world will be ablaze from flames that were started and fanned in the Middle East. But what we are seeing right now is a prototype—a trial balloon, if you prefer—as Satan practices and perfects his plan to bring all of mankind under his dominion. And whoever Satan cannot destroy in spirit, he will seek to destroy in body.

As I said earlier, war in the Middle East is raging as I write these words. I hope that a ceasefire will have been instituted by the time you read them. But even if the shooting has stopped, the uneasy peace will not last for very long. That is because satanic forces are at work in the region that will not quit stirring up trouble until they have been totally and eternally annihilated.

Anyone tempted at any time in the Last Days to think that a lasting peace has been struck would do well to remember the words of the apostle Paul as recorded in 1 Thessalonians 5:3: "While people are saying 'Peace and safety,' destruction will come on them suddenly, as labor pains on a pregnant woman, and they will not escape."

The underlying feelings that have led to the war in the Middle East will not die easily, especially because Satan keeps picking at them and doing his best to stir a bit more hatred and emotion into the pot.

Why was Saddam Hussein firing his Scud missiles at Israel, for instance, when Israel had nothing at all to do with the war? Innocent people were being killed in Tel Aviv, simply because of Hussein's unreasonable hatred of the Jews—a hatred that has been built within him by his lord and master, the devil, who hates all of God's people with a passion, and who reserves an especially cold place in his heart for the race through which the Messiah came. I know that some people would take issue with me, claiming that Saddam Hussein is a "religious" man, but his religion can have nothing at all to do with God.

Here is a man who has murdered anyone who even thought of standing in his way, including relatives and close friends. Recent news indicates that he has moved his anti-aircraft guns and other artillery into civilian neighborhoods, thus drawing enemy firepower down upon the heads of his own people. And it is reported that his army has set up "execution squads" to deal with soldiers who retreat from the front. Meanwhile, the soldiers who are on the front lines have almost no chance of survival, as they are pounded relentlessly by allied bombs and bullets.

Surely, if left to their own devices they would surrender and end this bloody conflict. But they cannot, simply because Saddam Hussein will not let them. One Iraqi prisoner of war reportedly told his captors, "If you want to end this thing, kill Saddam Hussein. Then the war will be over." Perhaps for now that is true. But were Hussein to fall, another despot would arise to take his place. Satan has no shortage of madmen anxious to do his will.

There can be little doubt that the leader of Iraq is a bloody, greedy, evil man. But he is really just another in a long line of such men that Satan has used for his own purposes. Each has been deceived with regard to his own importance in the scheme of things. Whether we are talking about Hitler, Khomeini or Hussein, each has considered himself to be a key player in the shaping of this planet's history. All of the others were used and discarded by Satan, and Saddam Hussein will be no different. He is serving Satan's purposes now, and then he will be tossed onto the eternal junk heap—or perhaps it would be more appropriate to say that he will be tossed into the eternal incinerator.

But make no mistake about it. When the Antichrist gets here he will make Saddam Hussein and his ilk seem like men of restraint and reason.

It can also be said about Saddam Hussein that, even though he is not going to be the central character in the drama that is about to take place, his appearance on the scene is most certainly evidence that the Last Days are approaching with the speed of a runaway freight train.

Bible scholars will tell you that the Book often makes use of "types." What that means is that some event or person is used to represent some other event or person. As the *American Heritage Dictionary* says, a type is "a figure, representation, or symbol of something to come, as an event in the Old Testament foreshadows another in the New Testament." I believe that Saddam Hussein is very much a type of one who is to come after him. I believe, further, that as we look at recent events in the Middle East, we can have a clearer understanding of some of the events foretold in the book of Revelation.

Likewise, to know what is about to happen on this planet of ours, the book of Revelation is the place to start. The fact that you are reading this book shows that you have an interest in seeing what God's Word says about the future. Perhaps that interest has been prompted by a lifetime of study and a personal relationship with God through Jesus Christ; or perhaps you are merely curious. Either way, know that the Bible alone has the answers, not only with regard to what events are about to occur, but also with regard to what is going to happen to you and me long after this planet of ours has been destroyed by fire. Other books may tell you the things you want to hear. God's book will tell you the way it is really going to be.

Let's take a chapter-by-chapter look at the Revelation of John—this amazing book that is as up-to-date as tomorrow's headlines. Along the way, we will see numerous ways in which the policies and attitudes of Saddam Hussein have paved the way for the fulfillment of the prophecies found in this last book of the Bible.

Now it is no secret that the Holy Bible is the best-selling book of all times. Every year millions more are sold, and every time a new translation comes out, whether it's the New King James, the New International, or any other version, it's not too long before we find it on the bestseller lists.

And that's good.

But while millions of people are discovering the wisdom of the ages within the pages of the Bible, many others have Bibles around the house and never even think of opening them to find out what is inside. Their Bibles sit on shelves gathering dust, or lie on coffee tables unopened—the Word of God serving as nothing more than a decoration.

And that's bad.

Because these people don't understand that the Bible is not just a book to have around the house to keep up appearances. It is not a good-luck charm, nor is it an ancient curiosity. The

Bible is a living, breathing Book that is relevant to our everyday lives. And it also tells us what we can expect on this planet of ours in the very near future.

Not too long ago, all of Southern California was in an uproar. A fifteenth-century "prophet" by the name of Nostradamus had predicted that California would be destroyed by an earthquake in May 1988. (At least that's what those who had studied his writings had come to believe.)

As May came around, some Californians were about to go into cardiac arrest, and others actually packed up and left the state. When the month passed without incident, some folks breathed a deep sigh of relief. Others, quite frankly, were disappointed.

We live in a society that wants to know what the future holds. It doesn't matter if it's good or bad—people just want to be prepared ahead of time. And so they pore through the writings of Nostradamus, or look into Edgar Cayce, or read those ridiculous predictions in the *National Enquirer*. Others give thousands of dollars to those who claim to "channel" for wise and ancient spirits; and even Nancy Reagan, it was said, wouldn't make a move without consulting her favorite astrologer.

Nonsense! All nonsense!

Meanwhile, the one Book that can really tell us what the future holds—the Bible—is left to sit silently, its wisdom unheard and unheeded.

Even those who do read and believe the Bible often shy away from the very book that speaks most dramatically to us today— the book of Revelation. I hear it all the time:

"Oh, I've given up on Revelation. I just can't understand it."

And, "Isn't Revelation supposed to be a sealed book? I mean, isn't it supposed to be hard for us to understand?"

No, Revelation is not supposed to be some sort of sealed, secret knowledge, too deep for mere mortals to grasp. Nor is it really that hard to understand. As a matter of fact, the very purpose of the book is to make clear to Christian believers the events that are due to happen on this earth when the end times arrive.

And now is the time to discover what Revelation has to say—because the end times have arrived!

This book is designed to help you understand the book of Revelation so that you will know what God is doing on the earth. I want to cut through all of the nonsense and get right to the truth.

You see, God is just about to pour out His judgment upon this world of ours. Anyone aware of what is going on knows that this world is in trouble. If you want to be prepared, if you want to be safe when the storm really breaks loose, if you want to see the spiritual realities behind today's headlines, then you need to know what God has to say in this, the last book of the Bible.

The very first chapter of the book says that it is the Apocalypse of Jesus Christ. *Apocalypse* is a Greek word meaning, literally, "the unveiling." And so the Apocalypse of Jesus Christ is literally the "unveiling" of Jesus Christ. It is in this book that Jesus unwraps the future for us, so we know what is going to take place on the earth.

When I was a boy, I lived in the pleasant little city of Ventura, California, which grew up around the San Buenaventura Mission, founded by Father Junipero Serra in the eighteenth century. On one occasion, the city of Ventura hired a sculptor to make a statue of Father Serra that was to be placed in front of City Hall. When the big day came for the unveiling of the statue, the folks around Ventura made quite a fuss about it—understandably they were proud of their city, and of this man who played such an important part in its history. It seemed as if the whole town turned out for the unveiling, and I was as proud as anyone else, especially since I was a member of the elementary school orchestra and we were playing at the ceremony.

There was the statue, covered with a huge white canvas. A

crane was poised above it, ready to remove the covering. I sat in the violin section, fidgeting impatiently while the mayor, the members of the county board of supervisors, and various Roman Catholic dignitaries all made speeches.

Finally the moment came, and the big crane whirred into action. Slowly—ever so slowly—the canvas began to lift. First we could see the pedestal, then the feet, the bottom of the priest's robe, and then—Father Junipero Serra—the founder of our city standing there in the sun, in all his glory! It was a breathtaking moment!

Well, the book of Revelation is an unveiling of gigantic proportions. A drama of cosmic ramifications is unfolding, and this book takes the cover off so we can understand it!

Before going any further, let me offer a bit of historical perspective about the book and its author.

I am sure you know that Revelation was written by the apostle John. And remember that this man had been very close to Jesus Christ during the Lord's three-year work on earth. He had been standing nearby when Jesus died on the cross and he was one of the first to know when Jesus was resurrected from the dead. Christ thought so much of John that from the cross He directed this "disciple whom He loved" to take His mother, Mary, into his home and treat her as his own mother.

All of those events took place many years before John received this final revelation from God. But even though he was probably in his mid-nineties when he had this vision, the fire of John's passion for his Lord had not dimmed in the least. He was the last survivor of the original twelve apostles, all of the others having been martyred long before—put to death by the Roman government for spreading a "subversive" new religion, Christianity.

One historian, Eusebius, tells us that John, too, was to have been martyred—boiled in oil, in fact—but God had other plans for him. We don't know if John was ever placed into boiling oil, or if his sentence was commuted, but he survived because God wanted to give him this final revelation regarding the earth's future.

So now he has been exiled to the island of Patmos, a rocky little crag out in the Mediterranean, not far from Ephesus, to live out the rest of his days. But he knows he is not alone here. God is with him.

The first verse of the book says that Jesus Christ made this revelation known by sending His angel to John. So for the most part the book consists of things this angel revealed to John—sometimes verbally and sometimes by showing visions of things that were to come.

At other times, John seems to have communicated directly with the Lord Himself, or had visions of the Lord.

Regardless of the means by which the author received the message, the book of Revelation presents a unified picture of things that "must shortly come to pass."

In verse two John states that he is merely recording what he has witnessed. He is not elaborating, exaggerating, or making things up. He is merely serving in the role of reporter, passing on what he has seen with his own eyes and heard with his own ears.

You may or may not remember anything about World War II. But you have probably heard of the broadcasts Edward R. Murrow made from the city of London, or you may have heard recordings of them. The war seemed distant to those who were safe in America, far away from the bombs and the sounds of enemy aircraft droning overhead. But Murrow's broadcasts, directly from the scene of beleaguered London, showed this country that the war was real, and that we were engaged in a struggle with the forces of evil.

In the same way, the apostle John is telling us in Revelation that a war is raging. It is real, and we had better wake up to that fact.

He is saying, in effect, "There are things about to happen in this universe—things that will have a tremendous impact upon all of you. I hope you are listening to me, because I know what I am talking about!"

Most of these revelations came to John by way of visions, which are simply insights into the world of the spirit. They are not mystical hallucinations in which we see things that don't really exist. Rather, they open our eyes to see things the way they really are.

In the book of 2 Kings, the Bible tells the story of what happened when the prophet Elisha and his servant were surrounded by enemy troops. The frightened servant was convinced that he and his master were doomed. How could they fight against such tremendous odds?

But when Elisha prayed, God opened the servant's eyes, and he saw that the troops who surrounded them were in turn surrounded by the armies of God. The fact that he couldn't see God's soldiers with his natural eyes didn't make them any less real. It was only when God allowed him a glimpse of the spiritual realm—a vision—that he understood the true nature of the situation.

Today's headlines point to a spiritual reality—namely, that we are living in the last times pointed to by the book of Revelation. But most people cannot see the spiritual reality behind those news stories. In this sense, they have no vision, and the Bible says in Proverbs 29:18 that the people will perish where there is no vision.

Visions may also have wider dimensions, as when God dramatically allows one of His people to see not only what is going on in the spiritual realm, but what has happened in the past, is happening in the present, or will happen in the future.

This is possible because the spiritual realm is eternal and timeless. There is no way, this side of eternity, to explain exactly what that means. One of the best illustrations I have heard is that all of history is like a giant reel of film, which we can see only one frame at a time.

If that film were stretched out in front of us, and if we could stand back and see it from that perspective, we would be able to see all of the scenes at the same time. If we looked at the beginning, we could see the creation of the universe. If we looked at the end, we could see the end of the world and the beginning of eternity. If we found the portion of the film that contained our own lives, we could see everything about ourselves, all at once.

The idea of a stretched-out film illustrates the way God is able to see the universe. He sees the whole thing—past, present, and future—at once, and He can show any portion He chooses to whomever He chooses at any time.

This is one way God can prove that He is eternal and dwells outside of time—by telling of things that will happen hundreds and sometimes thousands of years in the future. In Isaiah 44 God challenged the false gods to show things that were to come. Jesus said to His disciples that He was telling them things before they happened so that when they did happen, they might believe that He was the Messiah (see John 13:19).

The book of Revelation is John's recording of the portions of the "film of history" that God allowed him to see. Admittedly, there are portions of this book that are difficult to understand. John himself undoubtedly didn't understand the total significance of everything he saw, nor did he know with certainty when all of the things he recorded would begin to happen.

Remember, now, I didn't say John's Revelation is *impossible* to understand. If that were the case, God would never have given John the visions in the first place, nor would He have instructed the elderly apostle to write down everything he saw and heard. It is God's desire that we read, study, and come to understand this message. Concerning the prophecies of Daniel, for example, Jesus said, "Whoever reads, let him understand" (Matthew 24:15, NKJ).

Understanding will help God's people remain strong during times of struggle and persecution. It will remind us that everything is a part of God's plan, that we have not been forgotten or abandoned. It will also prepare us for what lies ahead, so that we will not be caught by surprise.

Beyond that, in the third verse of the first chapter, John—rather, God speaking through John—promises that whoever reads the book will be blessed. Therefore, if we read and study the book of Revelation, we are going to be blessed, and if we avoid it, we are missing out on a blessing from the Lord. It's really that simple. The promise of God's blessing is reason enough to learn what this book has to say.

Some people misunderstand Revelation because they see right away that John has addressed it to seven specific churches in Asia.

"If it was written to those churches," they say, "then it must not have that much to do with me today."

That attitude overlooks the symbolic nature of much of the book. After all, there were many more than seven churches in Asia during the latter part of the first century.

Why would John single out the seven mentioned in this book, and not say a word to some of the other equally prominent congregations of the Lord's family? We know that there was a church at Galatia, for instance, which had been established by the apostle Paul, and another congregation at Colosse, which received one of Paul's epistles.

Did these seven churches have special importance that set them apart from and above the others? No, not at all.

God has given the number seven a special significance. It is the number of completion and maturity. In many instances this is also true in the natural realm. There are seven days in a week, for example.

In the book of Revelation, we will find the number seven repeated several times to signify the completed nature of God's work in the universe. In this instance, the seven churches are used to signify that the message is for the complete Church—for all of God's people, in every country and in every age.

I saw a story in our local newspaper recently that made my

heart sink. It's the sort of story I have seen many times before, and I am sure I will see again.

Two young men were using an aluminum ladder to trim some branches from a tree. They apparently became so involved in their work that they forgot to be careful with the ladder and brushed it up against a power line. A tremendous jolt of electricity surged into them both, killing one instantly and injuring the other severely.

This tragic loss of a life could and should have been prevented. The men knew the power line was there; they could see the warning sign erected by the power company. But they simply didn't pay any attention to it.

This is the case with the book of Revelation. It is God's warning of what is about to happen on this planet of ours. We can choose to ignore it, but that won't change one thing that is about to happen.

And anyone who chooses to ignore the warnings sounded within this book does so at great personal risk.

The Key to the Book

Before we move further into the book of Revelation, take a look at the nineteenth verse of the first chapter:

> Write, therefore, what you have seen, what is now and
> what will take place later.

This command given to John actually divides the book of Revelation into three sections:

1. The things that John saw—the vision of Christ as recorded in the first chapter of the book.

2. The things that are, which deal with the messages to the seven churches in Asia in the second and third chapters.

3. The things that shall occur in the future, or, as it says in

the original Greek, "after these things." (When we get to the fourth chapter of Revelation, we will find that John once again uses these words, as a voice from heaven tells John that he is about to see what must take place "after these things.")

There are three specific schools of thought with regard to this book:

Historic—Adherents to this school of thought interpret the book as a history of the Church's struggle against man's government, beginning in the Roman period and extending on up through the present time.

Spiritual—This interpretation insists that everything recorded within Revelation is nothing more than spiritual allegory. It has spiritual significance, but it doesn't really pertain to anything that is happening physically anywhere within the universe. This is the most confusing way to view Revelation, and it also strips the book of much of its message, since every man is free to interpret the allegory as he sees fit.

Futurist—The futurists are those who believe that much of this book is a prophecy, that it is telling us about events that are going to be unfolding upon this planet of ours. I believe this is the correct view. The futurist believes that Revelation says what it means and means what it says, and he or she does not need to twist its words to make them fit any particular doctrine. The futurist believes this book is to be taken at face value, and his belief is supported by Revelation 1:19.

The futurist understands that to look into the book of Revelation, from chapter 4 on, is to look into the face of the future.

2

Just Around the Corner

Revelation 1–3

In the opening chapter of this book, we talked about Saddam Hussein, and the fact that his appearance on the world stage is very much related to the soon coming of the Antichrist.

Just who is this Antichrist? Is he the exact opposite of Christ Himself?

No, that would be impossible. Christ is the eternal Son of God, one Person of the Holy Trinity. The Antichrist will be Satan's attempt to equal the glory of Christ, but in a negative, evil way. That is an impossibility, because the glory of Christ can never be equaled.

The book of Revelation has a great deal to say about the coming of this Antichrist, and we will be discussing this event as we proceed through the book. We will also take a look at some of the characteristics of the Antichrist himself. But we must first make no mistake about the fact that the Antichrist, whatever he accomplishes, will be no match for the power and glory of Jesus and His Church. Furthermore, as powerful a world leader as this evil person will be, those who stand against him through the power of the blood of Christ will be gaining an eternal victory.

While the devil, in his limited power, can never be a true equal to God, his traits are certainly opposite to God's. Whereas God is pure goodness, the devil is pure evil; whereas God is always faithful, the devil is always unfaithful; whereas

God cannot tolerate a lie, the devil cannot tolerate the truth. We could go on and on. Still, God has no equal in power or majesty, and neither is there any force of equal strength arrayed against Him.

God is the all-powerful, omniscient, omnipresent Creator of the universe. Satan is merely one of God's created beings. He was once an angel of great power and rank, but because of his own pride, he led an unsuccessful rebellion against God, was stripped of his power and privilege, and has spent the rest of his career seeking revenge. That career is rapidly approaching its close, and to a great extent this is what the book of Revelation tells us about.

Satan is powerful, but his power is quite limited. He is fighting for all he is worth against the end he knows is coming for him—namely, eternal damnation. As the time for his annihilation draws closer, his fury increases and he does everything within his ability to rain destruction down upon everyone within his reach.

We will be talking more about this as we go along, but I think it is important to understand that he can in no way ever hope to stand up to God almighty. This is important because reading Revelation can be a pretty frightening experience, especially as we find out what is going to be happening on our planet in the very near future.

But through it all, we can remember that God is still very much in charge. Satan will do everything within his power to destroy, but his power is absolutely meaningless in the face of God's might. Whatever Satan means for your ruin and destruction, God can and will turn to your eternal benefit, if you trust Him and lean on Him.

Now, again, very soon there are going to be some strange and terrible things happening on this planet of ours.

How do I know? Because the Bible tells me so.

The sun will grow hotter and scorch the earth with intense heat. There will be a drought so terrible that it will cover the entire planet, without a drop of rain falling from the sky over a three-and-a-half year period. The seas will be so polluted that all life in them will die. New strains of disease will develop, leaving much of the world in torment. And mutant varieties of poisonous insects will wreak havoc on much of the population.

Does all this sound crazy? If it does, check today's newspaper headlines. Especially those coming from the Middle East, where Saddam Hussein has shown clearly that he puts his own personal career above anything else. He would not hesitate to destroy us all if by doing so he could maintain his own position and power.

We have witnessed this time and again. Here is one example. When the Exxon tanker *Valdez* ran aground, several million gallons of crude oil were spilled into the waters of Alaska's Prince William Sound. Understandably, there was a tremendous public outcry over this ecological disaster, and the Exxon Corporation was the focus of much public protest and anger. The captain of the *Valdez* was even made to stand trial, being charged that his negligence was largely to blame for the accident.

Yet no one suggested, even for a moment, that the captain had run the ship aground on purpose, or that dumping oil into the sound was anything but a tragic accident.

And yet, one of Saddam Hussein's battle tactics involved pumping oil from a major Kuwaiti refinery directly into the Persian Gulf. Hussein's personal oil spill dwarfed that of the *Valdez* before the allied forces were finally able to put a halt to it by crushing the pipeline with a few well-placed bombs.

How will that single act of Saddam Hussein affect the ecological balance of the Persian Gulf? No one can say for certain as I write this what the lasting effects will be. But scientists all agree that tremendous damage has been inflicted on the wildlife of the area, including several important species of fish. If the Allies had not acted to stem the flow of oil, it is quite possible that all of the marine life in the area could have been killed.

That didn't happen, but the potential was there. Hussein had it within his power to do something terrible, and his conscience did not keep him from trying it. Revelation tells us, as we will soon see, that a worldwide marine disaster is going to happen. As I said before, consider Saddam Hussein to be a dress rehearsal for the one who is to come after him.

Now regarding Hussein's conscience, neither did he have enough of one to refrain from using chemical and biological weapons against his own people.

We have seen the photographs—dozens of Kurdish villagers lying dead in the streets, including tiny children cradled in the arms of their mothers who were desperately trying to shield them from Hussein's poison gas. As I write this, he has not yet used chemical weapons in his war with the allied forces, but it has been reported that his top scientists are searching for a way to combine chemical weapons with their Soviet-built Scud missiles. The use of chemical and biological weapons would certainly be one way that several of the prophecies we are about to study could be fulfilled.

It has also been reported that Hussein has considered setting fire to major oil refineries in Kuwait as a means of thwarting allied attempts to liberate them. If that were accomplished, scientists say, it would send up a cloud of smoke so thick as to obscure the sun from view—not only in the Middle East, but all the way around the world. They say that such a large amount of smoke in the upper atmosphere could actually change the planet's weather—possibly even plunging us into the middle of a nuclear winter in which the sun would "hide its face." Hundreds of thousands of people would starve to death as farmers lose their crops to lack of sunlight.

Some of these scenarios sound like something out of science fiction, I know. The fact that they really could happen makes them seem more frightening, and brings events recorded in the book of Revelation closer to us. We either have developed or are developing the terrible technologies capable of bringing about the horrors that the apostle John foresaw nearly 2,000 years ago.

Not all of the calamities that are about to befall the earth are going to be the result of madness by some despot such as Saddam Hussein. Yes, some of them will result from the insanity of an evil world ruler and the men who choose to follow him, but others will come about because of the ignorance of well-meaning men. Still others will be the result of the rebellion of nature, as this once-perfect planet begins to writhe in anger and anguish in attempts to rid itself of the sin and perversion with which mankind has corrupted it.

What is going to happen, in all of this, is that man and nature will conspire together to bring about the purposes of God.

Everywhere we turn, scientists caution against the many ways we humans are turning this world against ourselves. We are polluting our waterways and our atmosphere, thereby burning huge holes in the ozone layer, which protects us from deadly ultraviolet rays.

Other scientists issue warning after warning about the "greenhouse effect," which they contend is gradually warming the atmosphere. The heightened temperatures, they say, will eventually melt the polar ice caps, resulting in worldwide flooding. They will also bring drought and wipe out much of the world's agriculturally productive land.

Have you heard about the killer bees? Swarms of this vicious strain of stinging insect, developed in South America, are winging their way northward year by year.

I'm sure you have heard enough, but let me bring up one other new and deadly enemy: AIDS.

As I write this, AIDS is considered by the American people to be our nation's number-one health problem. Thousands of people—most of them homosexuals or intravenous drug-users, but others, innocent victims—have been afflicted with AIDS in the last decade and very few of them have survived beyond three or four years, once it goes into Stage Two. There is no doubt that AIDS is a deadly killer.

The World Health Organization says that almost all of Africa is suffering through an AIDS epidemic that threatens to decimate entire countries. World Vision, the Christian relief agency, recently issued a statement saying that "Uganda has AIDS," meaning that millions of people in that small country either have the disease or have tested HIV Positive, an indication they will develop the disease in the future.

And yet, not many years ago, if someone mentioned AIDS, you figured they were talking about a dietetic candy, not a dreadful disease. The sudden emergence of AIDS as a worldwide threat to life is terrifying, and there are other diseases lurking just around the corner that will be even worse.

The Bible talks about all these coming catastrophes and says they will begin to happen when this planet is just about ready to pass into a transition that will bring an end to the present world system and the beginning of the Kingdom of God.

There is a way of escape, however, that God will provide to people all over the world who are part of His Church. They will be taken away from the earth just as these terrible things begin to happen. The book of Revelation is written to the Church, to warn her, to make her ready, and to comfort her with the knowledge that she will be spared when the worst of all times come upon the earth.

I mentioned before that many people misunderstand the book of Revelation because they find, in the first two chapters of the book, that its message is directed primarily to churches in seven specific Asian cities.

What they don't understand is that these seven particular churches are representative of the Church's entire history, the people of God of every country and every age.

Another misconception arises when people fail to understand that the Church consists of all the people of God—those who have been called out from the world, who have given themselves over to God, accepting the Lordship of Jesus and the gift of salvation offered through His death, burial, and resurrection. These people are being addressed in the book of Revelation. They need to be aware of what is about to happen so they can help spare others from the dangers that are about to befall this planet.

There have been many other times throughout history when God has spoken to warn His people of impending doom. For an example, consider the case of Lot. The angel warned Lot of the impending doom of the city of Sodom and led him out to safety, telling him that they could not destroy the city until he was safely out. Jesus told His disciples that a day was coming when Jerusalem would be destroyed and not one stone of the Temple would be left standing upon another. He told them that when they saw Jerusalem surrounded by the armies, they should flee to the mountains (see Luke 21:20–21).

That day arrived in 70 A.D. when Roman soldiers, led by General Titus, annihilated the city, killing thousands of its residents in the process. Interestingly enough, as far as we can tell, there were no Christians among those who were slaughtered by the Romans. Why? Because they knew what was coming. They listened to the warning of Jesus, and they continued to meet together, encouraging one another, and looking for signs of the destruction that they knew was sure to come.

They listened to the prophets who were among them and, just before Jerusalem fell before the Roman sword, fled into the nearby countryside, where they and their families were spared.

God Always Gives a Warning

God is concerned about His people and He wants to spare them from harm. When destruction is on its way, He offers warnings, but He doesn't force anyone to believe the message or act upon it. When the Great Flood was about to destroy all life on the face of the earth, God told Noah to preach to his friends and neighbors and warn them. But they wouldn't listen, and only Noah and his family, out of all the people on earth, survived.

When I tell some people that the message in the book of Revelation is intended for the Church, they immediately run up a barrier and refuse to listen.

"If it's connected somehow to the Church, then I don't want anything to do with it."

It's not hard for me to understand where that attitude comes from. It's sad but true that the Church does not have a history that inspires confidence and admiration.

During the history of the Church, Christians have killed Jews and have often been at war with other Christians. Catholics have killed Protestants and Protestants Catholics, all in the name of doctrinal purity. Protestants have killed other Protestants because of disagreements over the correct method of baptism. In our more recent history, church leaders have twisted the Scriptures to condone slavery, or at the very least racial bigotry.

Even today we read about the violence in Northern Ireland, and discover that its people are still divided along religious lines.

I would be the first to admit that the Church's history is often shameful. That's because the people who make up the Church are not perfect. They're ordinary human beings, just like you and me.

As the bumper sticker says, "Christians aren't perfect, just forgiven."

When John sat down on the isle of Patmos and wrote the book of Revelation, as directed by the Spirit of God, the Church was already falling far short of the ideal God intended for her. And so we find two things in these early chapters of the book:

1. A reminder of God's love for the Church.

2. A warning that certain changes are necessary.

Now I don't care much for people who go around spouting clichés all the time and claiming to be original thinkers, but I hope you will indulge me just this once. People who reject the message of the book of Revelation simply because they are troubled by the history of the Church are guilty of throwing out the baby with the bathwater.

The Church may not be perfect, but the One who founded the Church is. Jesus Christ is the same today as He was nearly two thousand years ago when He gave this message to His apostle John. He is perfect. He doesn't lie. And if He said something is going to happen, it is flat-out going to happen, guaranteed, no question about it.

You don't have to believe what any representative of the Church tells you. You certainly don't have to believe what any particular denomination says. And it won't bother me for a minute if you don't want to believe a word Chuck Smith says.

But if I am repeating what Jesus Christ said in His Word, then I'm telling the Truth with a capital T. If Jesus said it, you can stake your life on it.

One of the things that was happening to the Church in the latter part of the first century was that she was growing complacent.

Right after Jesus had been resurrected and ascended into heaven, the early Christians thought the end times were going to arrive any day. We can't blame them for their anticipation. Even though the Scriptures say that no one knows when Jesus will return, some of these people had seen Him ascending into the sky, and it was only natural that they expected Him to return soon. There was even a rumor going around that Jesus had promised He would return before the apostle John died—a rumor John did his best to dispel in the last chapter of the Gospel that bears his name.

But as the years went by and Jesus did not return, some Christians began to lose their faith. They began to return to the old habits and sins they gave up when they first came to know the Lord. Their passion for Him began to cool.

This happens to many Christians. When they first surrender their lives to Christ, they live in a world of excitement and anticipation. They look up at the moon and feel close to the One who created it. All of the world seems to hum with the refrain, *Jesus is coming back, and He's coming back soon.*

But as the days and weeks go by, the anticipation dies down.

The new Christian begins to think, "Jesus is coming back, sure, I know that's true. But He's not coming tonight, or tomorrow, or even this week. He's coming someday, but it's probably going to be a long wait."

This complacency may be compounded when he or she begins to realize that many people throughout history have come to believe they could pinpoint exactly when the Lord would return.

The Jehovah's Witnesses, for example, thought the world was sure to end in 1914. When it didn't happen, they moved the date up a few years. Then they said that something significant did happen in 1914—something that signified the beginning of the end, only it happened in heaven instead of here on earth.

In more recent times, the Witnesses picked 1975 as the year the Lord would return. Wrong again.

A well-meaning Christian wrote a well-publicized book in which he explained why the Rapture would occur in September 1988. He had 88 reasons to support his contention, and backed up his claims by the fact that he was a former NASA engineer, accustomed to solving complicated mathematical mysteries. He was certainly well-intentioned—including about his revised prediction of September 1989, when September 1988 came and went—but he was also wrong.

I have no doubt that many Christians were convinced by his arguments, and I have heard stories about some who put their pets to sleep, not wanting their animal friends to be abandoned when they were raptured. I have also heard of people who ran up tremendous debts in the early part of 1988, assuming that they were going to be raptured, and the "heathen" would be stuck with the bills. I don't know if those stories are true—and I hope they're not—but I do know for certain that many people were hurt and some may have lost their faith when the Rapture did not occur on this man's schedule.

These are two instances in which people thought they had God's plan all figured out, only to wind up looking like fools, or worse. Unfortunately these people are like the little boy in the fable who kept crying, "Wolf!" One day, the wolf actually did show up, but nobody would believe the boy's report.

I know, given the many wrong expectations over the centuries, that it may seem naïve for me to be saying now that I am convinced we are in the end times. But the truth is that there are some compelling biblical reasons to believe this is so. The signs are all about us.

Anyone who presumes to give a specific date must be regarded with skepticism. God never promised us that we could put a big circle around a specific date on the calendar, marking it as the day of Christ's return. But He did give us specific guidelines that will tell us as that day approaches.

Jesus Himself said that when He returns He will come like a thief in the night—but because of all the erroneous predictions and false prophets, there will be many who will disregard the legitimate signs of His coming.

Not only are Christians growing complacent, but nonbelievers are scoffing at the signs that point to the fact that we are living in the end times. I have had them tell me, "The world is exactly the same today as it's always been."

They can trot out newspaper headlines from 100 years ago that prove that man was just as depraved then as he is today. They cite violence, hatred in the world, and just as many reasons—or so it would seem—for religious people to have believed that this old planet was on its last legs.

What they don't see, though, is that there are other biblical signs to let us know when we are nearing the end of the world as we know it. The Bible is clear in its warning that no one will know the exact day or hour when Jesus will return, but it is just as clear in its assertion that believers will be able to see certain things happening and know that the return of Jesus Christ is at hand.

Jesus Himself said, in the twenty-first chapter of the Gospel of Luke, "When you see these things happening, you know that the kingdom of God is near" (verse 31).

The prophet Daniel quoted an angel as telling him this about his vision of the end times: "Go your way, Daniel, because the words are closed up and sealed until the time of the end. Many will be purified, made spotless and refined, but the wicked will continue to be wicked. None of the wicked will understand, but those who are wise will understand" (Daniel 12:9–10).

In other words, just because a few people have been wrong in their efforts to pinpoint the exact day of the Rapture, or of Christ's return, doesn't mean that we should give up in our efforts to know whether or not we are living in the last days. The Bible itself states that the wise will see the signs and know when those days arrive.

Those signs are all around us now, indicating that this present age will soon be drawing to a cataclysmic close.

One of the most important signs is the rebirth of the nation of Israel foretold in Ezekiel 36–38, and that rebirth as related in time to the last days. Jesus said that when Jerusalem fell to Rome, it would be trodden down by the Gentiles until the times of the Gentiles were fulfilled (see Luke 21:24). In 1967 Jerusalem ceased to be a divided city and came fully under the control of Israel.

Paul tells us in 1 Thessalonians 5:4, moreover, that we are not the children of darkness, so that this day would not catch us unaware. Declared Jesus:

> Now learn this lesson from the fig tree: As soon as its twigs
> get tender and its leaves come out, you know that summer
> is near. Even so, when you see all these things, you know
> that [the Son of Man] is near, right at the door.
>
> Matthew 24:32–33

Before discussing more fully what lies just ahead for this planet, let me set the stage by discussing John's messages to the seven churches in the second and third chapters of Revelation.

I have already stated that these churches are representative of the universal Church. Actually, there is more to it than that. Each of these seven churches, I believe, also represents a particular period of Church history. For instance, the church at Smyrna represents the Church of the second through fourth centuries—a time when persecution was horrible and as many as six million Christians were executed for their faith. The church at Pergamum represents the beginning of the church-state system that developed under Constantine. And so on. I will explain in more detail as we continue.

Ephesus

The Ephesian church is commended for the hard work she does ceaselessly in the name of Jesus.

This is a tremendously active church, one where all the committees are functioning as they are supposed to. The auditorium is full to overflowing each Sunday, and the Sunday school is bursting at the seams. There's undoubtedly a perpetual building program underway here.

But something is wrong.

This church has forgotten her first love. She has forgotten that what the Lord longs for is people who love Him and want to serve Him out of that love. The Ephesian church is busy trying to substitute hard work for a loving relationship with

God. And that's what He wants most of all—a loving relationship with you and me.

At one time the church of Ephesus was on fire for the Lord. Her love for Him had launched all these marvelous programs in the first place. But over a period of time, that flame of love began to flicker and die. All of the wonderful programs are still there—only now nobody can quite remember why.

There are many Christians in the world today who are members of the Ephesian church. Somewhere along the line their ardor has cooled. They used to talk about the Lord all the time. They may even have been annoying to others because they couldn't seem to hold a conversation without bringing Jesus into it. But those days are gone.

What is God's message to the Ephesian Christians?

"Repent," He says. "Rediscover and rekindle that love you once felt for Me. If you don't, I will remove you from My presence."

Jesus will not stay where there is no love.

In God's economy, love is the most important commodity. To see just *how* important, turn over to the thirteenth chapter of 1 Corinthians and see what the apostle Paul has to say about it:

> If I speak in the tongues of men and of angels, but have not love, I am only a resounding gong or a clanging cymbal. If I have the gift of prophecy and can fathom all mysteries and all knowledge, and if I have a faith that can move mountains, but have not love, I am nothing. If I give all I possess to the poor and surrender my body to the flames, but have not love, I gain nothing.
>
> 1 Corinthians 13:1–3

It is interesting to note that the Ephesian Christians do find favor in the eyes of Christ because they hate the deeds of the Nicolaitans, which He also hates.

Just what were the Nicolaitans doing that was so bad? They were attempting to add extra steps between God and man. Their attitude was one of, "Look, there's just no way you can go directly to God. He is too great, too powerful, in fact, too busy, to deal directly with you."

And so they built up a hierarchy: "You can bring your requests to So–and–So, who will in turn take them to So–and–So, and on up the ladder, until they will finally come before the throne of God." This bureaucratic structure was also guilty of trying to exercise control over people's lives well beyond the authority of the holy Scriptures.

Remember, when Jesus Christ died, the veil in the Temple in Jerusalem was torn from top to bottom. This meant that man now had direct access to God. From that day to this, no man has needed any intermediary between himself and God other than the Lord Jesus Christ.

First Timothy 2:5 tells us that "there is one God and one mediator between God and men, the man Christ Jesus."

This is not to say that there isn't a legitimate authority structure in the church. A pastor has responsibility for looking after the spiritual welfare of his people. But he does not have the authority to tell them how to conduct their everyday affairs, nor can he attempt to set himself as an indispensable link between them and God.

Any religious leader who attempts to tell his flock whom they can or can't marry, what sort of car to drive, where they ought to live, or who seeks to exercise lordship over his people deserves a swift kick to his posterior—delivered in love, of course!

Smyrna

The second church mentioned in the book of Revelation is the one at Smyrna. Whereas the Ephesian church represents the Church as it existed up until the deaths of the apostles, Smyrna represents the Church of the second and third centuries . . . the Church that went through such terrible persecution at the hands of the Roman government.

Millions of Christians were executed during this time. Some were fed to the lions, others were stretched out on racks, and thousands were put to death in mass crucifixions as the Romans sought to eradicate Christianity.

The message to the church of Smyrna, then, is one of comfort and encouragement. Jesus reminds us here who He is, how He suffered and died Himself, but was resurrected. He says:

> "Be faithful, even to the point of death, and I will give you
> the crown of life."   Revelation 2:10

Pergamum

Whereas the Christians of Smyrna were being tortured and killed by the governmental authorities, the church at Pergamum was safer physically but was threatened spiritually, for it was co-opted by those same authorities.

This is a church trying to join the world's system, attempting to build a church-state structure in which righteousness is brought into existence through legislation. It simply can't be done.

When the Emperor Constantine declared Christianity the official religion of the Roman Empire, he meant well. But in reality, he was strangling the life out of the Church. God has never intended for His Church to be a part of the world's political system in any age—including the present one.

Christ has encouragement for the church at Pergamum because the Christians here have remained true to His name. In contrast to Smyrna, however, which hated the deeds of the Nicolaitans, we find some here who have embraced those deeds. These people are urged to repent before God deals with them harshly.

Jesus also promises to give a white stone to the Christian who overcomes. In those days a white stone was a symbol of acceptance, and a black stone the symbol of rejection. (Hence the term *blackballed.*) Jesus is saying, in essence, that He will accept whoever is able to overcome.

Thyatira

What Jesus is doing, here in the second and third chapters of Revelation, is pointing out what must be corrected to prevent His judgment from falling on the Church throughout the various stages of her history and development.

In the beginning of this message, Christ has some very positive things to say about the church of Thyatira. He knows her works, her charity, her love, her service, and her faith. But then He says that this church has been practicing immorality and has been "eating meat that has been sacrificed to idols."

It seems to me that this message is addressed to the Roman Catholic system, and to the way that this system developed in Church history prior to the Reformation. I do not mean to pick on the Roman Catholic Church, and you will see that as I talk about the next church, the church of Sardis, I apply the harsh words of judgment regarding that church to Protestant Christians. But the message to the church of Thyatira seems to pinpoint some specific problems within Catholicism.

When Jesus accuses the church of eating meat that has been sacrificed to idols, I think He is referring to the relics and images that have been introduced into its worship. Objects to be kissed or prayed to may have been intended to be stepping-stones to God, but instead they have become objects of worship themselves.

It is interesting to note that Jesus commands the faithful in this church to "hold onto what you have until I come." In other words, this church system will be in existence up until the time

Christ returns to take His believers home with Him.

But it is important to remember that He calls His people within this church to repentance, to a "turning away" from idols, and warns that unless they do repent, they will pass through the time of suffering that is coming upon the earth.

Sardis

And now we come to the Protestant Reformation.
What does Christ say?

> "I know your deeds; you have a reputation of being alive, but you are dead. Wake up! Strengthen what remains and is about to die, for I have not found your deeds complete in the sight of my God."   Revelation 3:1–2

This is the church that professes to believe in Jesus Christ, but attempts to explain every miracle of the Bible in natural terms. This church has forgotten the power of God.

This church may pride herself on being set free from restraints, hierarchy, and formal liturgy, but it hasn't replaced these things with anything better. It looks upon a liturgical church as formal, cold, and dead, when it might as well be looking in a mirror and pronouncing those judgments upon itself.

When Christ says that the works of the church at Sardis are not complete, He is also saying that this church has accepted into her system much of the idolatry of the Roman system— idolatry borrowed from the religion in Babylon that should have been denounced and set aside.

Want an example? What about Christmas?

Christmas, although used to celebrate the birth of Christ, actually comes out of an ancient Babylonian festival in honor of the winter solstice. The ancients knew that this was the time of year when the days stopped growing shorter and began to grow longer again, and they developed a religious festival that was actually a drunken, debauched celebration. This festival was adopted by the Romans, given the name Saturnalia, and gift-giving was added to the drunkenness and feasting.

The Roman Catholic Church incorporated the festival into its calendar, stating that Christ was born on that day. The truth is that scriptural evidence indicates that He was probably born sometime during the fall, although we don't know the exact day.

Christmas, then, is only one of the many pagan festivals incorporated into the life of the Roman Catholic Church, and then brought into the Protestant Church.

Should Christians stop celebrating on December 25? Not at all. We enjoy glorious liberty as children of God to celebrate or not to celebrate, as we choose. Any celebration should focus, however, not on parties or gifts—that would make us no better than pagans ourselves—but on the Word become flesh who dwelt among us.

In Sardis, despite the incorporation of idolatry, there are those who walk with the Lord, dressed in white, whose names will not be erased from the Book of Life.

Philadelphia

The sixth of the seven churches to which the book of Revelation is written is the church at Philadelphia. This is the church that has held fast to the faith, seeking to please the Lord in all she does.

These people are serious about Christianity. They are the true believers who allow their faith to color every aspect of their lives. They're looking for Jesus to return, and they want to be ready.

One of the most exciting things that Christ says to this church, as far as I am concerned, is this:

> "See, I have placed before you an open door that no one
> can shut."   Revelation 3:8

He goes on to say,

> "I know that you have little strength, yet you have kept
> my word and have not denied my name."

The Lord has set before His Church an open door of opportunity, and nobody will ever be able to shut it.

As long as we are looking for ways to further God's Kingdom, for souls to win, and for opportunities to serve, we will find them. And we will find them in spite of our weakness.

In Revelation 3:10, Christ also makes this promise:

> "Since you have kept my command to endure patiently,
> I will also keep you from the hour of trial that is going to
> come upon the whole world to test those who live on the
> earth."

I doubt if the Lord could have said it more clearly. Yes, there is a time of severe trials coming upon the earth—and not just part of the earth, but the entire planet. But you, because you have been faithful to Me, He says, will be spared.

Most serious biblical scholars who are also believers agree that a time of tremendous tribulation will come upon the earth before the end of this age. But there are sharp disagreements over when this Tribulation period will take place, and what the Church's role in it will be.

Some point to what is happening to Christians in Eastern European countries and say, "It looks like the Tribulation has already started over there. And if those people have to suffer, who are we to think that we're going to escape?"

And so you hear people talking about whether there will be a pre-Trib, mid-Trib, or post-Trib Rapture. In other words, will God's people be taken out of the world before the Tribulation begins, during the middle of it, or after it's over?

No one is in spiritual danger because he doesn't hold to the correct doctrine about the Rapture. This is not one of the central tenets of the faith, such as a belief in the atoning death of Jesus Christ. At the same time, I believe with all my heart that the Bible teaches that the true Church of Christ—the people who cling to God's Word and do their very best to serve Him—will be taken out of this world before the Tribulation really begins.

This doesn't mean that there won't be any believers on the earth during the time of Tribulation; I'll talk more about that later on.

Neither does it mean that we who are Christians now won't have to pass through some difficult times. It has always been the lot of Christians to suffer for their faith. Jesus said to His disciples, "In this world you will have trouble" (John 16:33). Again: "If you belonged to the world, it would love you as its own. As it is, you do not belong to the world, but I have chosen you out of the world. That is why the world hates you" (John 15:19).

Faith in Jesus has always entailed personal sacrifice and always will. But making sacrifices or being persecuted because of what we believe in is not the same as passing through the Tribulation. Neither is suffering the consequences of living in a fallen world.

Do Christians get sick and die? Yes, they do.

Do Christians sometimes find themselves in financial difficulties for reasons beyond their control? Or course they do.

Are Christians victimized by burglars, robbers, and other criminals? Again, the answer is yes.

Christians get the flu, stub their toes, get toothaches, and are laid off from their jobs, just like anybody else on this planet.

But the Tribulation has not yet started—and if you think the things discussed thus far are terrible, all I can say is, "You ain't seen nothin' yet." A time is coming, very shortly, when God's wrath is going to be poured out upon the earth, and if you as a believer are doing all you can to serve the Lord, you won't be here to see it.

Laodicea

Now we come to the last of the seven churches. This church, the church of Laodicea, is in for a rude awakening. She is smug and arrogant in her self-confidence, believing she serves the Lord, when in reality she serves only herself.

This church is fat and rich with her roots firmly entrenched in the soil of this planet. She has lost her eternal perspective and grown cold and indifferent. In her early days God began to bless her, but after a while she took her eyes off God and began to seek only the blessing.

And then, somewhere further along the line, she even forgot where her original blessing had come from—the hand of God— and began to believe that she had brought these blessings upon herself through hard work and diligence.

This church may have erected ornate cathedrals, sanctuaries with huge stained-glass windows, and/or successful publishing and broadcasting empires. But she is lukewarm.

Jesus says:

> "Because you are lukewarm—neither hot nor cold—I am
> about to spit you out of my mouth."   Revelation 3:16

Are you a member of the Laodicean church? Somewhere along the line, have you lost your zeal and your passion for God? You still believe, but it's just not the way it used to be?

If so, there is a remedy for your situation. Christ says that if you will open the door, He will come in and commune with you. Invite Christ back into your life. Tell Him you want to serve Him. Ask Him to restore your passion. He will do it and then you, too, will be missing from this planet when the terrible day of Tribulation finally dawns.

In Revelation 1:19, the key verse for the entire book, John was told that he would write about "the things which will take place after this" (NKJ). After what? After the things of the Church. And so the second and third chapters of Revelation have taken us completely through the era of the Church. It is important to note that these two chapters have taken us to the Second Coming of Christ and the great Tribulation.

We have seen the failures of the Church and her strengths. There has been error and apostasy. There has been lukewarmness and a loss of first love.

But through it all, there has been a continuous thread of true believers—those who have remained faithful to Christ and who have sought to serve Him in word and deed.

As we come to the end of the third chapter of Revelation, the Church is about to pass from the scene. And that means that the earth will be making her final, shaky orbits around the sun.

The Rapture is at hand.

3

The Day of Redemption Draws Near

Revelation 4–6

As we turn to the fourth chapter of Revelation, we turn toward the future, for these are "the things which will take place after this [after the Church things]" (Revelation 1:19, NKJ). We now look at the post-Church world.

Perhaps you've seen the bumper sticker that reads, *Warning! In case of Rapture, this car will be driverless.*

It may have made you grimace as you pictured hundreds of suddenly driverless cars careening down an expressway.

Well, let me assure you that it really is going to happen someday—and my feeling is that a great many people who are now alive will still be alive when it happens.

You may also have seen paintings of the Rapture, showing hundreds of people rising into the air, coming out of the windows of tall buildings, rising through the roofs of cars, and so on. Dramatic? Yes, but this does not represent my own understanding of what is going to take place when the Rapture occurs.

If millions of people all over this earth suddenly rose straight up into the air, physically, there would be no way to deny what had happened. This would be an obvious miracle of staggering proportions, and even the most adamant unbeliever would have to admit that something "supernatural" had happened. But the Bible indicates that even after the Rapture, life on this planet will continue on in much the same old way. Apparently there will not be total turning to God because of the Rapture, and so it will happen in such a way that its divine origins will not be immediately obvious.

I think the *spirits* of those who are raptured will ascend into the skies to meet Jesus, and not their physical bodies. At the moment of the Rapture, our spirits will take flight, shedding our physical bodies like so many beautiful butterflies leaving their cocoons. Paul said, "The perishable must clothe itself with the imperishable, and the mortal with immortality" (1 Corinthians 15:53). For as he pointed out, "Flesh and blood cannot inherit the kingdom of God" (verse 50).

Those who don't know God, then, will be able to report the incident as a worldwide plague that has mysteriously taken millions of lives overnight. Scientists will investigate the event and probably come up with one or two "natural" explanations.

They won't understand that God has raptured His people to spare them from the troubles that are about to come upon our planet.

I believe the Rapture is going to happen because God said it will and He never lies. When the Bible says something, we can believe it. I know from personal experience—after many, many years of walking with God—that He always does exactly what He says He's going to do.

What is the biblical basis for believing in the Rapture? Well, for one thing, Jesus talks about it in Matthew 24:37–42:

> "As it was in the days of Noah, so it will be at the coming of the Son of Man. For in the days before the flood, people were eating and drinking, marrying and giving in marriage, up to the day Noah entered the ark; and they knew nothing about what would happen until the flood came and took them all away. That is how it will be at the coming of the Son of Man. Two men will be in the field; one will be taken and the other left. Two women will be

grinding with a hand mill; one will be taken and the other left.

"Therefore keep watch, because you do not know on what day your Lord will come."

The apostle Paul also talks about the Rapture in 1 Thessalonians 4:16–17:

. . . And the dead in Christ will rise first. After that, we who are still alive and are left will be caught up together with them in the clouds to meet the Lord in the air. And so we will be with the Lord forever.

And again, in 1 Corinthians 15:51–52, he says: "Listen, I tell you a mystery: We will not all sleep, but we will all be changed—in a flash, in the twinkling of an eye. . . ."

There's one more very important verse to consider, and that is found in 2 Thessalonians 2:1–7:

Concerning the coming of our Lord Jesus Christ and our being gathered to him, we ask you, brothers, not to become easily unsettled or alarmed by some prophecy, report or letter supposed to have come from us, saying that the day of the Lord has already come. Don't let anyone deceive you in any way, for that day will not come until the rebellion occurs and the man of lawlessness is revealed, the man doomed to destruction. He will oppose and will exalt himself over everything that is called God or is worshiped, so that he sets himself up in God's temple, proclaiming himself to be God.

Don't you remember that when I was with you I used to tell you these things? And now you know what is holding him back, so that he may be revealed at the proper time. For the secret power of lawlessness is already at

work; but the one who now holds it back will continue to
do so till he is taken out of the way.

I believe the last part of this Scripture is the most intriguing
and relates most directly to the subject at hand. The Phillips
translation puts verses 6 and 8: "You now know about the
'restraining power' which prevents him from being revealed
until the proper time. . . . When that happens the lawless man
will be plainly seen."

Who is this lawless man, this "son of perdition"? The Antichrist, the one whose appearance on the scene will signal the
beginning of the end. But he won't come until that which is
holding him back is removed from the scene. And what is it
holding him back?

The Holy Spirit, operating through the Church of Christ.

As long as the Church is here, the Antichrist will be powerless. He may be alive in the flesh somewhere on earth right now.
In fact, I think odds are pretty good that he is. I wouldn't
pretend to know where, or what he's doing. He's most likely
masquerading as an ordinary citizen, slowly gaining in influence and popularity on a local scale. On a worldwide level, he
is nothing at all.

But as soon as the Rapture occurs and the Church is out of
the way, watch out, because the restraining power of the Holy
Spirit will be removed, and all hell is going to break loose.

It is not only that the Antichrist will come upon the scene,
but the beginnings of God's wrath will be poured out upon the
earth as well.

Yet people will still fail to recognize the hand of God at work
on the earth. God could write across the face of the moon in
big block letters *Repent and be saved,* and there would be those
who failed to see anything supernatural about it. They can't see
God's hand in anything, and they never will—until it's too late
for them.

I wonder about these people every time I see a baby, or smell a rose, or take a walk along the beach. How could anyone observe these things and not know there's a God behind it all? And yet we have people around us who believe that all the beautiful things about us are nothing more than the result of blind chance. How can anyone see a beautiful little girl, running and laughing with her hair flying behind her, and say she exists only because of fortuitous occurrences of accidental circumstance that put the gears of evolution into motion in some slimy swamp millions of years ago?

And yet that's exactly what they say. As God declared, "Although they claimed to be wise, they became fools . . . and worshiped and served created things rather than the Creator" (Romans 1:22, 25). Thus, because they won't see God in the sparkling eyes of that little girl, they won't see Him anywhere else either—including the Rapture.

And then there will be those who do believe, but who won't admit it. Why? Because they will have pledged their lives to the Antichrist. They will know right from the beginning what he is really planning to do, but they will disguise their true motives in talk of worldwide peace and unity. Even now, they may be plotting their strategy to divide and conquer the world.

And so, as soon as the Church is out of the way, the world will be divided into two angry and warring camps.

There will be those who come to believe in Christ after the Rapture has occurred. On the other side will be all the non-believers, along with those who pretend not to believe. When the believers begin to question the true motives and aims of this "great new world leader" who is really the Antichrist, his supporters will shout them down and point to his many "accomplishments" in the name of peace, harmony, and brotherhood.

And what is in store for those who come to believe in Christ only after the Rapture already occurs? Unfortunately it will be too late for them to escape the terrible things that are going to be happening, although God can and will make a distinction between His people and those who do not belong to Him. This means that His people will not always suffer as the nonbelievers will, but it will be a terrible time nonetheless—a time of "natural" disasters on the earth, and a time of persecution and martyrdom at the hands of the Antichrist and his followers.

The Heavenly Throne

Revelation 4 is transitional. Here we change from the earthly scene to the heavenly, and move from the things that take place during the history of the Church on earth to those things that will transpire once the Church has been transferred to glory.

John, speaking as a representative of the Church, sees a door open in heaven and hears a voice "like a trumpet" inviting him to come up into the heavenly scene to view the future.

Two other New Testament passages we have just looked at mention the sounding of the trumpet with specific reference to the Rapture: 1 Corinthians 15:52 and 1 Thessalonians 4:16. This being so, and since the Thessalonians passage also mentions the voice of the archangel, many Bible scholars believe that Revelation 4 marks the event of the Rapture.

It is noteworthy that we read no mention of the Church being on the earth after this event until she returns with Christ to establish His reign. Rather, the Church is seen in heaven—in Revelation 7:9–10, for example, praising God for salvation.

The first thing that catches John's attention in heaven is the awesome sight of God sitting on His throne:

> And the one who sat there had the appearance of jasper and carnelian. A rainbow, resembling an emerald, encircled the throne. . . . From the throne came flashes of lightning, rumblings and peals of thunder. . . . Also before the throne there was what looked like a sea of glass, clear as crystal.   Revelation 4:3, 5–6

God is surrounded by the angels known as the cherubim and 24 elders sitting on lesser thrones.

The Old Testament prophet Ezekiel records a similar vision of the throne of God:

> Above the expanse . . . was what looked like a throne of sapphire, and high above on the throne was a figure like that of a man. . . . Like the appearance of a rainbow in the clouds on a rainy day, so was the radiance around him.
>
> Ezekiel 1:26, 28

Ezekiel records a second vision of God's throne with the cherubim in chapter 10. Isaiah spoke of a similar vision in chapter 6 of his book. And Daniel describes the heavenly throne in chapter 7.

John, in rapt attention, hears the beautiful worship of God by the cherubim and watches the response of the 24 elders as they lay their crowns before the throne. Their words declare the worthiness of God to receive the glory, honor, and power that have been ascribed to Him, for He is the Creator of all things and the object of creation: All created things exist for His pleasure.

Here is an important philosophy of life. You and I as created beings exist for God's good pleasure. We may fight against this truth. We may feel it isn't fair that God should create us for His own pleasure. And we may live so as to please ourselves. In this event, however, we will discover that life lacks purpose and fulfillment because we are not answering the basic purpose of our existence.

If, on the other hand, we live to please God we will find our lives as David described when he declared, "My cup runneth over" (Psalm 23:5, KJV). Our cups of life will not only be full but running over. As Jesus said: "Whoever wants to save his life will lose it, but whoever loses his life for me will find it" (Matthew 16:25).

The Breaking of the Seals

In chapter five of Revelation, we have a glimpse of what will be going on in heaven as the Tribulation is about to unfold.

> Then I saw in the right hand of him who sat on the throne
> a scroll with writing on both sides and sealed with seven
> seals. And I saw a mighty angel proclaiming in a loud
> voice, "Who is worthy to break the seals and open the
> scroll?" But no one in heaven or on earth or under the
> earth could open the scroll or even look inside it. I wept
> and wept because no one was found who was worthy to
> open the scroll or look inside.   Revelation 5:1–4

Why was John sobbing about this? Had his curiosity gotten the best of him? Was he afraid?

To understand John's reaction, as well as the idea of being "worthy" to break the seals, we have to understand something about the way real estate transactions were handled in ancient Israel.

Whenever a Jew sold a parcel of land or lost it through forfeit, the transaction always included a "redemption" clause. The seller of the land had a right to buy it back within a specified period of time, providing he could fulfill the terms and requirements that were written into the deed.

When property changed hands in this way, two deeds were drawn up. One was sealed and put away in a safe deposit box. The other remained open and was retained by the person who sold the property.

Later on, if the person who had sold the property decided to buy it back, both deeds would be brought to the table. The one who wanted to "redeem" the property would use the open deed to prove that he had the authority to do so. Then he would break the seals of the other deed, fulfill the requirements listed therein, and the property would revert to his ownership.

If he was unable to fulfill the requirements necessary to redeem his property, one of his relatives could do it. If he couldn't do it, and none of his relatives could do it, the land was lost to him forever.

In Jeremiah 32 there's a recounting of an incident in which the prophet was thrown into prison by an angry king because he had prophesied that Jerusalem was going to fall to the Babylonians. In the meantime, the Babylonian army had come against the city, and it must have been obvious to nearly everyone that Jeremiah was going to be right.

In the middle of this situation Jeremiah's cousin Hanamel asks Jeremiah to redeem a field for which he as a kin had the right of redemption. Jeremiah might have said, "What are you talking about? Don't you know we're about to be conquered by the Babylonians, and they're going to carry us off into seventy years of captivity? What would I possibly want with your land?"

He could have said that, but he didn't. Instead he redeemed the land and had the two deeds put into a jar and buried, so he could use the property. He redeemed the land as a symbol of faith in God. In effect, he was saying to the people, "We will lose this land of ours for a while. But we will come back someday. It's not gone forever."

So what is this scroll in the right hand of God? It's a title deed. A title deed to the earth.

You see, originally the earth belonged to God. After all, He is the One who created it, so why shouldn't it belong to Him?

But when God created man, He turned ownership of the planet over to him. Look in the first chapter of Genesis, and we find God telling man to take dominion over the earth, to subdue it, to take charge over it.

But no sooner does man begin his task than he defaults on the whole deal and turns things over to Satan. He turns his back on God, disobeying His command not to eat of the tree of the knowledge of good and evil, and obeying Satan's suggestion that he eat (see Genesis 3:1–19).

Satan has had this planet under his control ever since—and that's why things are in such a mess.

At this point, some of you are afraid I'm bordering on blasphemy. I have had people ask me, "What are you talking about when you say this world is under the control of Satan? He was defeated at the cross."

Yes, it is true that Satan was defeated when Jesus Christ died, was buried, and rose from the grave, but he has yet to lay down his arms and surrender. What Jesus did will bring ultimate and complete victory over Satan, but we have not yet received the entire benefits of His acts.

We may sit in church and sing the hymn "This Is My Father's World," and in a technical sense, that's true. But in our present age, the world is still under Satan's control, and he still thinks he can defeat God, despite what Jesus did on the cross.

The apostle Paul called him the god of this world. And Jesus Himself referred to Satan as the prince of this world. We see that the world still belongs to Satan in Revelation 13:2, when he gives it to the beast who rises out of the sea, who is the Antichrist. Concerning the redemption of the world through Jesus, Hebrews 2:8 tells us that God put all things in subjection to Him, although we do not yet see all things put under Him.

In the fourth chapter of Matthew, we find the account of Satan's temptation of Jesus just prior to the time when Christ began His ministry. In one of those temptations, Satan took Christ up into a high mountain and showed Him the cities and kingdoms stretched out beneath them.

Then he said, in effect, "Just look at all of this—and all of it belongs to me. If You'll only bow down and worship me, I'll give it all to You."

Jesus didn't say, "What are you talking about, Satan? This doesn't belong to you, but to the Father."

No, Jesus didn't argue with the devil over who had ownership of all these kingdoms. He knew very well that Satan was currently in control. He also knew that He had come to redeem all this for His Father, but that this was not the way to go about it.

If Jesus Christ had, for one moment, bowed His knee to Satan, the eternal battle would have been over and the evil one would have won the victory.

Jesus Christ was going to redeem the world, and He was going to do it by the shedding of His blood. Without Jesus' death and resurrection, there is no way this world could ever have escaped Satan's clutches.

This explains what John sees taking place in heaven. Not one person can be found to break the seals on the deed to the earth and thus restore the planet to its rightful owner, God almighty. But then Jesus Christ, the Lamb who was slain for the sins of the world, comes forward, and He alone is able to break the seals and redeem the property.

> Then one of the elders said to me, "Do not weep! See, the Lion of the tribe of Judah, the Root of David, has triumphed. He is able to open the scroll and its seven seals."
>
> Revelation 5:5

This heavenly scene hasn't taken place yet, but I believe it is going to happen soon. There are several reasons for believing this. And if we take another look at the Old Testament laws regarding redemption of property, we see an interesting parallel.

Whenever a piece of property was sold, the original owners had a set period of time—usually seven years—in which they had to redeem it if they wanted to regain possession. If the property was not redeemed, it remained under new ownership.

This seven-year period also applied to a man who was sold into slavery. During the seventh year of his service, he was to be offered his freedom. If he didn't want his freedom, his owner took steps to show that he would remain a slave all his life.

I think it is more than coincidental that it was just about six thousand years ago that Adam and Eve disobeyed God and sold the world into slavery. According to biblical chronology, it was roughly 4,000 B.C. when Adam first ate of the forbidden fruit. That means the world is coming very close to entering the "seventh year" of its captivity. This seems significant. And although no one knows the date of Christ's return, we can, as Jesus said, "know that summer is near" (Matthew 24:32). In this regard, I believe that the scene of redemption as previewed by the apostle John will be occurring very soon—within the next 25 years at the maximum.

There is not a man alive who could ever begin to redeem the world, and that's true in spite of what the politicians tell us. Every four years in this country, we have a presidential campaign during which we listen to two men—and sometimes many more than that—who tell us they've got this whole thing figured out. "Vote for me and my party, and we'll rid the world of all its ills and put it back the way it's supposed to be."

They tell us that they're all for "traditional values" and "strong moral character," and everyone applauds and thinks that one or the other of them will put us back on the right track. In 1988, the American people decided George Bush was the best man for the job.

Well, while George Bush may be a fine President, no one can redeem this nation, much less the whole world, aside from the Lord Jesus Christ.

In Revelation 5 John continues to record the scene he has observed:

And I looked, and behold, in the midst of the throne and of the four living creatures, and in the midst of the elders, stood a Lamb as though it had been slain, having seven horns and seven eyes, which are the seven Spirits of God sent out into all the earth. Then He came and took the scroll out of the right hand of Him who sat on the throne. Now when He had taken the scroll, the four living creatures and the twenty-four elders fell down before the Lamb, each having a harp, and golden bowls full of incense, which are the prayers of the saints. And they sang a new song, saying: "You are worthy to take the scroll, and to open its seals; for You were slain, and have redeemed us to God by Your blood out of every tribe and tongue and people and nation, and have made us kings and priests to our God; and we shall reign on the earth."

Revelation 5:6–10, NKJ

This is what Jesus referred to in Luke 21 when He warned about the great Tribulation that would come upon the earth. To His disciples He said, "Watch ye therefore, and pray always, that ye may be accounted worthy to escape all these things that shall come to pass [i.e., the things of the Tribulation], and to stand before the Son of man" (verse 36, KJV).

This is just what we see pictured here in the heavenly scene in Revelation 5, as the four living creatures and the elders sing of the Church's redemption through the blood of Jesus, and the wrath of God is about to be poured out upon the earth.

And so the Lamb, who has been slaughtered, comes forward, takes the scroll from the hand of God, and begins to break the seals, thus restoring the world to God's control.

This is ultimately very good news for the earth, but as the seals are broken, the righteous judgments of God begin to be poured out upon the planet.

As the first seal is broken, John tells us that he hears a voice that sounds like thunder telling him to come.

> I looked, and there before me was a white horse! Its rider held a bow, and he was given a crown, and he rode out as a conqueror bent on conquest.   Revelation 6:2

Who is this rider? None other than the Antichrist, coming forward in Satan's last-ditch effort to regain control of the earth and all the people living on it.

Note that he comes forward on a white horse, looking for all the world like a good guy, a savior. He's bent on nothing less than the destruction and enslavement of the entire human race, but most people won't realize this until it's too late.

Now I have talked to people who were living in Germany during the rise of Adolf Hitler, and I have asked them how a man as evil as he was could have assumed power in that country.

And you know what? Most of them had had no idea what sort of person he was.

He came across as a hero—someone who would restore the pride of the German people, who would rebuild the country's shattered economy, who cared about the common man. Hitler appealed, in fact, to those who wanted a return to old-fashioned morality and who believed that men and women deserved a chance to succeed through hard work.

Meanwhile, however, he was busy trying to exterminate the Jewish race from the face of the earth, crushing the weak and defenseless wherever they were found, and involving not only his beloved Germany but the entire world in a war that would cost millions of lives.

More recently, consider Saddam Hussein. Throughout much of the Arab world, he is regarded as a hero even though his career has been spectacularly bloody and ruthless.

It is reported of Hussein that immediately after becoming

president of Iraq in 1979, he launched a brutal purge. Dozens of top government officials were accused of plotting against him, found guilty in hasty trials and executed.

One of the more famous stories about him concerns a cabinet meeting held during the summer of 1982. During that period, Iraq was at war with Iran and an invasion of Baghdad appeared to be imminent. It was reported that one of Hussein's cabinet members, Riyadh Ibrahim, suggested that Saddam step down temporarily to pave the way for a cease-fire agreement.

Without showing the slightest trace of irritation, Saddam invited his colleague to go into another room to discuss the matter further. The minister agreed and the two men left the room together. A few moments later, a gunshot rang out, and Hussein returned to the regular cabinet meeting alone. Riyadh was found dead, with a bullet hole in his head. The official story was that the minister had been executed for distributing tainted medicine.

When Iraqi minister of defense Adnan Khairallah Talfah disappeared in 1989, the official explanation was that he had been killed in a helicopter crash after he had flown into a sandstorm.

Those who knew of Hussein's ruthlessness found that explanation difficult to believe. They knew that the Iraqi president had grown increasingly uneasy over Talfah's popularity. They also were suspicious that Iraq was suddenly losing more of its leaders through helicopter crashes during peacetime then it had lost during the entire war with Iran.

The Antichrist will be brutal to an extent that Saddam Hussein cannot even imagine. But, in spite of this, he will be hailed as a hero, and millions throughout the world will see him not as someone who has come to destroy, but as the leader for which the world has been waiting.

As the second seal is broken, another horse rides out over the earth, a fiery red one whose rider has the power to take peace away and bring war upon the planet. So we see that a horrible time of war is about to come upon the earth.

The breaking of the third seal sends forth a black horse with a rider holding a pair of balances in his hand.

As this horse rides out, John hears a voice saying:

> "A quart of wheat for a day's wages, and three quarts of
> barley for a day's wages, and do not damage the oil and
> the wine!"   Revelation 6:6

This horse signifies, then, that a famine is about to come upon the earth. A man will work all day and barely be able to purchase a small loaf of bread with the money he makes.

Just think about the famine in Ethiopia and other poor, drought-stricken countries, and imagine such devastation around the world. We've all seen the heart-rending news footage of starving children with distended bellies. We have died a little inside to see mothers with sunken eyes and bony arms reaching out in desperation for whatever bits of food might be offered.

The day is coming, though, when those scenes will be commonplace right here in America, even in the wealthiest areas of our cities.

Now if you want to be rich during the time of Tribulation, I have a plan for you: Go out, buy up all the wheat you can find, and store it away. I guarantee that when the Tribulation gets here, you'll be one of the richest persons in the country. And once it's over you might possibly be the richest person in hell!

I think it's significant that the horse and rider bringing famine follow closely on the heels of the horse representing war. I believe that's because the war will feature the use of many powerful nuclear weapons. The fallout from such a war will render most of the world's crops inedible, bringing about worldwide famine and starvation as a result.

If we want to get an idea of what a nuclear war would mean in terms of the world's food production, we need only to consider what happened in Europe when the Chernobyl nuclear plant malfunctioned. Milk produced by cows as far away as Western Europe had to be poured out because it was contaminated with radioactive fallout. Farmers hundreds of miles from Chernobyl were forced to destroy their crops for the same reason.

And that was a relatively small accident from one nuclear reactor. If one incident could cause all that damage, then it's hard to imagine exactly what a full-scale nuclear war would do. Fortunately, those of us who belong to God's Church won't ever have to find out.

As the fourth seal is broken, another horse and rider come forth, and these, if possible, are even more terrible than the others.

> I looked, and there before me was a pale horse! Its rider was named Death, and Hades was following close behind him. They were given power over a fourth of the earth to kill by sword, famine and plague, and by the wild beasts of the earth.   Revelation 6:8

So there you have the Four Horsemen of the Apocalypse, riding out to bring God's terrible yet righteous judgment on a world that has chosen to turn its back on Him and scorn the only way He has provided for man's eternal peace—the shed blood of His only begotten Son, Jesus Christ.

One Billion Will Die

John tells us that by the time these four horsemen have finished their horrible ride, fully one quarter of the earth's population will have succumbed to war, famine, and plagues of various sorts.

Within recent times, the earth's population has climbed past the five billion mark. Assuming that twenty percent of these people are Christians, there will still be four billion people left on this planet after the Rapture takes place. Simple arithmetic tells me that one billion will die in the beginning of the Tribulation.

How many is a billion? The word has become so common that we fail to grasp the quantity it represents. Put into perspective, it's almost more than the human mind can comprehend.

Suppose we wanted to count to a billion, and we were able to count at the rate of one number per second. How long would it take? Well, it would only take a little over eleven days to make it to a million. That's a long time to be counting, but we're not through yet! We'd have to keep counting, and keep counting, and keep counting, for nearly 32 more years! That should begin to give us some idea of how many a billion really is.

Now try to imagine a billion human lives wiped out in a bloody whirlwind of war, famine, and pestilence. We can't comprehend the worth of one single life, so how can we begin to think of a billion people dying?

This planet of ours has seen some terrible times in the past. In World War I, more than ten million people lost their lives. It was a terrible tragedy, but people consoled themselves with the thought that it had been "the war to end all wars."

Yet it took just over twenty years for a new and even more terrible war to develop. This time, almost fifty million people died, and a high percentage of these were civilians, including the millions massacred by a monster named Adolf Hitler.

Many years have passed since that war ended, and we have largely forgotten the horror. We see pictures—of mushroom clouds rising over Hiroshima and Nagasaki, of bombed-out Berlin, of emaciated bodies stacked like so much firewood in death camp yards—and pictures can only make us shudder at the thought of living through such horrifying days.

But as terrible as those two World Wars were, they seem

almost insignificant when compared to the devastation that is just around the corner.

In 1984–85, much of the world's attention was directed toward Africa and, specifically, Ethiopia, where thousands of people were starving to death because of a prolonged drought. Millions of dollars' worth of aid poured into that country and the situation got better.

But there has been very little long-term or lasting progress in that region. Millions of people in Africa are living very tenuously. For them, one poor growing season would be disastrous.

The next major famine will not be confined to the continent of Africa; it will strike the entire world.

As soon as the Four Horsemen are on their way, the fifth seal is opened. And this time, instead of unleashing more tragedy upon the earth, John sees the souls of those people who had been martyred because of their faith in God.

> When he opened the fifth seal, I saw under the altar the souls of those who had been slain because of the word of God and the testimony they had maintained. They called out in a loud voice, "How long, Sovereign Lord, holy and true, until you judge the inhabitants of the earth and avenge our blood?" Then each of them was given a white robe, and they were told to wait a little longer, until the number of their fellow servants and brothers who were to be killed as they had been was completed.
>
> Revelation 6:9–11

Who are these people? Are they the ones who were killed during the earliest days of the Church, when the Roman government was routinely conducting mass executions of Christians? Or are they those who have died at the hands of regimes behind the Iron Curtain, or in countries like Uganda?

I believe, rather, that these are the souls of those believers who will have been martyred during the time of the Tribulation. The Bible tells us that when the Antichrist comes, he is going to be given the power to make war against the saints and prevail over them. What "saints" are we talking about here? It can't be the Church, because Jesus says in Matthew 16:18 that "the gates of hell shall not prevail against it" (KJV).

But once the Church has been raptured, the earth is going to experience one of the greatest revivals it's ever seen. People who have heard the Gospel message all their lives without giving it much thought will suddenly realize that it's true. Millions will drop to their knees and surrender their lives to Jesus.

Not all of these will remain faithful, as I have said before. But those who do hold onto the faith will do so in the face of severe and cruel opposition. Not only will the Antichrist be out to destroy them, but he will use all the public relations tools at his disposal to convince the non-Christian population that Christians are responsible for all the earth's troubles.

Think it can't be done? Just consider how Hitler helped to turn the German people against the Jews. Take a look at the Soviet Union, and its all-too-often successful policy of "disinformation." These new Christians are going to be among the most hated, most persecuted people on the face of the earth, and millions of them will be killed.

Part of this new distrust of Christians will come about because of a sudden burst of prosperity immediately following the Rapture. After all, the Christians aren't going to be able to take it with them when they go, so they'll leave everything behind for their unsaved friends and neighbors to divvy up. The Antichrist and his lieutenants will point to this newfound wealth and say, "See! It was the Christians who were holding you back all the time. Now that they're out of the way, look at how much better you're doing!"

The logical next step is for the message to become, "Just

think how well you'd be doing if these new Christians were out of the way as well."

As I said, this was the method employed in Nazi Germany, and it helped to bring a refined and cultured nation to the point of blind anger and prejudice against the Jews. Blame for everything that went wrong in the German economy was laid at the doorstep of the Jewish population. It's always nice to have someone to blame.

Another reason for the persecution of these new Christians is that they will know what the Antichrist is up to and seek to resist him however they can. Resistance to the new world ruler will not be tolerated and he will do his best to eliminate those who oppose him.

"These Christian must die," he'll say, "because they stand in the way of progress, peace, and harmony." He'll probably even shed a few crocodile tears over the fact that so many people have to die, but he'll keep promising that the end will justify this terrible means. He'll also promise to build a wonderful new world on the tears of these poor misguided souls who had to die.

"Wait a minute," someone says. "Non-Christians are still human beings. Will they stand by and let this happen?"

Sure they will, and we can see a striking parallel in the way Communism has spread in the twentieth century. Communism has caused the deaths of millions upon millions of people, all in the name of a coming Utopia, when the state will wither away and all people will live in peace and harmony. There will be no more war, no more hunger, no more suffering of any kind—and if the Communists have to kill fifty or sixty million people to bring that about, well, it's a small price to pay. Personally I've never understood how people who are so interested in lasting peace and brotherhood can be so ruthless as to torture and kill innocent people—but how very deceptive Satan can be! These soldiers of Communism somehow come to believe that the terrible pain and suffering they are inflicting now is going to do good in the long run.

And in John 16:2, Jesus said, ". . . A time is coming when anyone who kills you will think he is offering a service to God."

When the Antichrist commands that everyone everywhere accept his mark—I'll talk more about that later—these Christians will not be able to do it. This will single them out for persecution and torture.

In the coming age, the victims of holocaust will not only be Jews, but those who have turned to Jesus Christ after the Rapture.

And now, as the sixth seal is opened, John is witness to a great earthquake. And he reports that the sun turns black, the moon turns as red as blood, and the stars begin to fall to the earth.

> The sky receded like a scroll, rolling up, and every moun-
> tain and island was removed from its place.
>
> Revelation 6:14

He goes on to say that all the people of the earth, from kings and princes right on down to the poorest slaves,

> hid in caves and among the rocks of the mountains. They
> called to the mountains and the rocks, "Fall on us and
> hide us from the face of him who sits on the throne and
> from the wrath of the Lamb! For the great day of their
> wrath has come, and who can stand?"
>
> verses 15–17

As the sixth seal is broken, the very earth itself is shaken and its face changed.

Islands will be swallowed up by the sea. Mountains will crumble. And stars will fall from the sky.

Have you ever read stories about explorers finding tropical plants frozen in the ice of Antarctica? Did you wonder how they got there?

I have read that scientists found frozen carcasses of woolly mammoths in Siberia. One of the huge beasts had been eating when he suddenly died, and the plants he had been chewing on were still in his mouth. They were plants that could never exist in the icy Siberia of the twentieth century.

That's enough of a mystery in itself, but it's compounded when you try to figure out how the mammoths were so well-preserved—as if they had been flash-frozen.

One minute they were munching on tropical plants in balmy 80-degree weather, and the next minute they were encased in ice. How could it have happened? Did the whole world suddenly perform a flip-flop?

Some scientists think that's exactly what happened. And according to John's record in the book of Revelation, it may happen again.

When a Star Fell from the Sky

In the Arizona desert, near the city of Winslow, there is a huge hole in the ground called Meteor Crater. Scientists tell us that a meteorite slammed into the earth here thousands of years ago, leaving a hole nearly a mile wide and almost 600 feet deep. Upon impact, the meteorite also threw up a rim of rocks and soil that averages about 135 feet in height.

What does this have to do with the earth flipping on its axis? Maybe nothing. But maybe a great deal.

The meteorite that plunged into Arizona so many years ago was of sufficient mass to twist the earth and almost immediately place lands that had been subtropical under the polar icecaps. A shift in the earth's axis would also have brought about terrific damage as the earth's crust was twisted and torn. Mountains would have crumbled and islands would have disappeared.

The meteorite's impact would undoubtedly have pushed thousands of tons of dust and debris into the atmosphere. A dust cloud of such immense proportions, similar to that created by an erupting volcano, would change the earth's atmosphere. Looking through the dust and haze could darken the sun and give the moon the appearance of blood.

And, of course, there would be a tremendous earthquake at the moment of impact.

It may sound farfetched, but no one has ever come up with a more plausible way to explain the existence of those frozen mammoths with tropical plants in their mouths.

Now remember what John said will happen when the sixth seal is broken:

> There was a great earthquake. The sun turned black like sackcloth made of goat hair, the whole moon turned blood red, and the stars in the sky fell to earth, as late figs drop from a fig tree when shaken by a strong wind. The sky receded like a scroll, rolling up, and every mountain and island was removed from its place.   Revelation 6:12–14

Imagine the earth being bombarded by dozens of meteorites the same size or even bigger than the one that left that gaping hole in the floor of the Arizona desert. Think of the devastation it would cause.

This may or may not be what John is talking about here. Regardless, we can be sure that a dreadful calamity is going to befall the earth and all those living on it.

This is the day spoken of by the prophet Joel when he said,

> . . . The earth shakes, the sky trembles, the sun and moon are darkened, and the stars no longer shine. The Lord thunders at the head of his army; his forces are beyond

number, and mighty are those who obey his command. The day of the Lord is great; it is dreadful. Who can endure it?   Joel 2:10–11

Who can endure the day of God's wrath? Only those who are safely in heaven with Him when all this is taking place. I don't expect to be here on earth to see it happen. Neither should you if you give your life to God. We will be among those standing before God's throne singing praises to His name.

Christians can take comfort in the words of Paul, as recorded in 1 Thessalonians 5:9: "For God did not appoint us to suffer wrath but to receive salvation through our Lord Jesus Christ." And again in Romans 5:9: "Since we have now been justified by his blood, how much more shall we be saved from God's wrath through him!"

There is no doubt that the earth will pass through a terrible time and, as I have said before, I believe it will happen within the next 25 years. The good news is that there is a way of escape, and if you belong to Jesus Christ, you have already found it.

4

The Seventh Seal

Revelation 7–9

Driving through the California desert, just before you get to Palm Springs, you see them standing there like some strange contraptions from outer space, row upon row of them rising into the sky like so many gigantic soldiers.

Many miles closer, you see propellers attached to them, creating the appearance of huge and clumsy flying machines that can't quite get off the ground.

The first time I saw them, there were perhaps twenty or thirty. A year or two later, there were several hundred. Now there must be thousands.

What are they?

Windmills.

But not the sort of windmills you would expect to find on a farm in the Texas Panhandle. They're strange, imposing, space-age looking contraptions—the old windmill brought into the twenty-first century.

Why are there so many of them in the desert near Palm Springs? Because someone hit upon the great idea of harnessing the wind that blows through that area and turning it into electrical power. And so you have people investing their money in windmill construction and praying for windy days. They know that the windier the day, the more power the windmills will generate. And the more power there is to sell to local power companies, the bigger the return on their investments.

Now, I've driven through that part of the country a few times over the years, and I had never seen the wind as an opportunity. As far as I was concerned, it was a nuisance. First of all, the wind makes it harder to steer the car straight. You never know when an especially strong gust is going to hit you and nearly push you off the road. Secondly, sometimes the wind kicks up the sand and dust so that you can't see where you're going. I've seen cars come out of that area looking as though they have been sandblasted.

But I saw only the bad effects of the wind. Someone else saw it as an opportunity and took advantage of it.

I don't know what you think of the wind. You may view it as a nuisance that messes up your hair, blows important papers away, and plays havoc with the lawn furniture. Or, you may welcome it as a good excuse to take the kids out on a kite-flying expedition.

Whatever our opinions, we know that the wind is something God put on this planet to help us. And it's not going to be easy for anyone when, one day soon, the wind stops blowing altogether.

That is what's going to happen, according to the seventh chapter of Revelation, which says in the first verse that four angels will "prevent any wind from blowing on the land or on the sea or on any tree."

What would happen today if the winds stopped blowing?

For one thing, air pollution would become unbearable. Also, it would stop raining. The wind is part of the hydraulic cycle that produces rain, and thus helps to keep our planet alive. As ocean water is evaporated into the atmosphere, it is carried via the wind over the land masses, where it cools, condenses into clouds, and then falls to the earth in the form of rain. If there were no wind, the evaporated water would simply rise straight up into the atmosphere and remain there.

Wind may sometimes be a nuisance, but it's part of an important system that God has built into the earth. The people on this planet will find out just *how* important when He sends His angels to prevent it from blowing.

In fact, we'll see a bit later on that it is not going to rain on the earth for 42 months. Again my mind turns to the Southwestern desert, because I imagine that much of the world is going to be that dry, dusty, and barren before the 42 months without rain have come to an end.

As I write, those of us who live in California know that the state is entering its fifth year of drought. We have had some rain. Sometimes it has poured down. But we have not had as much rain as we need, and we are in trouble because of it. California is supposed to be "green and golden" but these days much of it is dirty brown.

Some counties have already instituted strict water rationing policies, and many others are soon to follow. We are bombarded with radio and television commercials reminding us to conserve water. I found it most interesting that California Governor Pete Wilson recently made the statement that the drought gripping our state was like "a biblical scourge."

Governor Wilson may be more accurate than he knows. I cannot help but wonder if nature is "practicing" on the 27 million people who live in California, for the real "biblical scourge."

Whether this is true or not, anyone who lives in California can tell you that when that 42-month dry spell comes, it will be anything but pleasant.

We'll talk more about the earth's dry period later on, but right now I have the feeling that some readers might think I've left something out.

"In the last chapter," someone says, "you were talking about the Lamb removing the seven seals from the scroll."

That's right.

"Well, you got down to number six, which brought about cataclysmic changes on the earth, and then you stopped. Now you're talking about the wind and rain being held back from the earth. What happened to the seventh seal?"

It's coming. But it will be so awesome that God will delay it for a short while. The earth will already be reeling from the breaking of the other seals, but now the wind will stop blowing and complete calm will reign. This is truly the calm before the storm, a time of preparation for what is just ahead, a brief period when God's wrath and judgment will be restrained.

The cessation of wind will be a relief at first, giving the world a chance to catch its breath. But as time goes by and the winds do not resume, earth's inhabitants will begin to worry.

And then, in Revelation 7:2–3, John reports:

> I saw another angel coming up from the east, having the seal of the living God. He called out in a loud voice to the four angels who had been given power to harm the land and the sea: "Do not harm the land or the sea or the trees until we put a seal on the foreheads of the servants of our God."

God is calling a time-out. It will be time for Him to work again with His chosen people. Those Jews who are still living on the earth but who have now accepted Jesus Christ as Messiah are going to be marked—singled out so they do not have to suffer the same fate as those who do not belong to God.

You may wonder how God will be able to spare His people from these terrible calamities. I don't know, but I do know that He is able to distinguish between those who belong to Him and those who don't.

For example, look at the plagues that fell upon Egypt when the children of Israel were in slavery there. (See Exodus 7–11.) Time and again those who belonged to God were spared—either because they had advance warning of what was coming, or because God put a supernatural shield around them. Either way, God made a distinction and they were protected while disaster raged all around them.

And so the angels go about the job of sealing those who belong to God, some 144,000 people "from all the tribes of Israel" (Revelation 7:4) who receive God's seal on their foreheads.

What sort of mark will they receive? I am not sure whether it will be something visible to the natural eye, or whether it will be a spiritual seal—but God will be able to see it.

There is a great deal of controversy and speculation regarding just who these 144,000 people will be.

Our neighborhood has a group of very zealous Jehovah's Witnesses. I admire their extreme dedication to their church. They are way off-base when it comes to what they believe, but they believe it with a passion. I wonder sometimes just how many doorbells they have worn out over the years.

The Jehovah's Witnesses believe that the 144,000 will be those from among their ranks who make it into heaven. The rest of them are going to inherit the earth—or so they believe.

Unfortunately for them those 144,000 won't come from Kingdom Hall.

Neither will they come from Herbert W. Armstrong's Worldwide Church of God. Subscribers to that church's teachings believe that if they give double or triple tithes, they have a chance to make it into this inner circle of 144,000. The Worldwide Church of God even promises to send these folks a telegram when the time comes so they can escape to the wilderness where there is a camp set up for their safety.

Many other groups have claimed that the 144,000 will come from among their ranks. But to believe any of these claims, you have to disregard the clear teaching of the Scriptures.

First of all, these 144,000 will not be raptured when the Church is taken from the earth, so they will not turn to God until after the Tribulation is well underway. Second, since these 144,000 will come from the various tribes of Israel, they are obviously part of the Jewish remnant that will turn to God during the last days of this planet. God is not yet done with His chosen people, the nation of Israel.

And while the 144,000 are being sealed, a great crowd in heaven will be worshiping God and praising Him for saving their souls.

These are the believers who will have lost their lives during the Tribulation because of their allegiance to God. In the middle of the terror that is happening on the earth, John says of these martyrs:

> "Never again will they hunger; never again will they thirst. The sun will not beat upon them, nor any scorching heat. For the Lamb at the center of the throne will be their shepherd; he will lead them to springs of living water. And God will wipe away every tear from their eyes."
>
> Revelation 7:16–17

No wonder these people will worship God with so much fervor, singing and shouting praises to His name!

And then the seventh seal will be opened. Immediately there will be a reverent silence throughout heaven, a realization that God is about to move in a tremendous way. All the singing and shouting and praising will stop, and everything will become deathly quiet for about half an hour. Everything will come to a sudden halt in anticipation of the scene that is about to unfold.

There are times when the Spirit of God begins to move, and a sudden silence sweeps over everything. An awareness of the majesty of God and His presence overwhelms you, and all you can do is drop to your knees and worship Him in silence. There is nothing you can say or do, because you are so struck by the reality of who God is and what He has done for you.

This, I believe, is what will happen in heaven as the seventh seal is opened. This will be a silence that speaks louder than any words ever could about the greatness of God, and about the events that are going to happen on the earth.

And then the fireworks will begin.

Whenever I read the eighth chapter of Revelation, I'm reminded of the kind of fireworks display you see on the Fourth of July. The first loud explosion paints the sky with dozens of brilliant colors and everybody gasps in appreciation. But before you have time to catch your breath, there is another brilliant display, and another, and another.

This is the picture we get of the seven judgments of God as they come bursting forth upon the earth. John tells us that he saw seven angels with seven trumpets, and as the trumpets are sounded, God's wrath is poured out.

As the first angel sounds his trumpet, hail and fire mixed with blood are hurled upon the earth.

> A third of the earth was burned up, a third of the trees
> were burned up, and all the green grass was burned up.
> Revelation 8:7

In Arizona, outside of Tucson on Kitt Peak, stands an observatory with several powerful telescopes. One of the main objects of research conducted at Kitt Peak is to chart the progress of asteroids that pose a real threat to the earth.

Some two thousand asteroids have already been identified as having orbits that could ultimately bring them into a collision course with the earth. These are not harmless specks of space debris. Some of them measure as much as 480 miles across.

Some scientists are actually discussing preventive measures to be taken if we should ever face immediate danger from an asteroid. Right now they're talking about sending a rocket armed with a nuclear warhead to destroy an asteroid whose orbit would threaten a collision with the earth. They believe a direct hit from such an asteroid a kilometer or so in diameter could cause the earth more damage than it would receive in a nuclear exchange.

You know that our planet spins as it travels through space. What would happen if a huge asteroid crashed into it? It might stop spinning, it might topple over, it might reverse its spin, but it would definitely not continue on the same steady course it had been following.

I'm not saying the chances are high that the earth will be hit by an asteroid. This year, scientists say our chances of suffering such a disaster are roughly three in a million. There's probably a better chance that Ed McMahon will walk up to your door and hand you a check for $10 million! But the chance is there, and those three-in-one-million odds don't take God's involvement into account.

The last time we had a close call with an asteroid was in 1937 when one came within 500,000 miles of the earth. That doesn't sound very close, but a slight change in direction or velocity could have sent it straight toward us.

Many scientists believe a collision with a much smaller piece of space debris caused massive destruction in Siberia in 1909. That year an explosion and fire toppled trees and killed all the wildlife in an area several hundred square miles in size. One minute it was a thickly forested part of the country, and the next minute it was barren and desolate.

No investigation has ever offered a 100-percent sure explanation of what happened there, but it could have been caused by impact with a "visitor" from space.

Sodom and Gomorrah Revisited?

If we go back in the book of Genesis to the story of Sodom and Gomorrah, we find that God destroyed those two cities by raining fire and brimstone on them. Could it be that these two evil places were wiped off the face of the earth when they were hit by huge meteorites or asteroids? Could it be that this is the first of the judgments that will occur when the seventh seal is opened?

It is entirely possible, of course, that this will be a spectacular, supernatural work of God—fire raining down from heaven to consume much of the earth. But I tend to think there will be some "natural" explanation behind it. That's why I believe God might use a "stray" asteroid or meteorite to carry out His plan. In this way, some of the survivors will see the tragedy as a judgment of God, and will turn to Him, but others will continue to say, "God didn't have anything to do with it. It's terrible, but there is a scientific explanation."

I have walked with God long enough to know that He often operates this way. I know people who have seen God intervene in their lives time and again—with healings, financial miracles, and many other sorts of blessings—and yet after each occurrence they have become skeptical regarding God's involvement.

"I don't know what God had to do with it," they say. "Sure I got a huge raise just when we really needed it, but I was overdue for a raise anyway." It takes a certain amount of faith to see God's hand at work. Those who don't want to believe in God or give Him any credit can always find a way out of doing so.

And now the second angel sounds his trumpet and

> Something like a huge mountain, all ablaze, was thrown into the sea. A third of the sea turned into blood, a third of the living creatures in the sea died, and a third of the ships were destroyed.   Revelation 8:8–9

This, too, sounds as if it could be caused by a huge asteroid or meteorite, flaming brightly as it plunges into what is probably the Mediterranean Sea.

What would result from such an event?

1. The initial impact would destroy sea life for miles around.

2. The resultant tidal wave would sink ships and devastate coastal cities.

3. Disintegration of the meteorite would pollute the sea. It's probable that this would result in a situation similar to a "red tide," in which much of the remaining sea life would die.

Remember, too, that Saddam Hussein brought about an ecological nightmare by dumping millions of gallons of crude oil into the Persian Gulf.

Reportedly, one of the things he planned to do was to set that oil on fire so that allied ships would have to stay far off shore. Now there was some debate as to whether that plan would have worked. Some scientists said that the oil would not burn if it were floating on top of ocean water. Others thought that it might. The possibility is a pretty frightening picture, isn't it— the ocean on fire? Surely it sounds like something from the book of Revelation.

By the time allied forces brought the slick under control it had covered some 350 square miles, and was threatening to close down desalinization plants that provide 95 percent of the drinking water for that dry, thirsty region. It was also threatening to shut electric power plants, industrial plants and agricultural projects, all of which require clean water for operation.

Whenever I see a photograph of the earth taken from space, I am always impressed by the deep, blue color of our planet. It looks like a sparkling jewel hanging in the blackness of space. And then I realize that that deep blue color comes from the fact that seventy percent of our planet is covered by water.

It is that water that provides us with so much of what we need for survival. Anyone who poisons the seas is, in reality, poisoning all of mankind. That is what will happen when the second angel sounds his trumpet.

And the destruction isn't over yet.

As the third angel sounds his trumpet, a great star falls from heaven, "blazing like a torch" (verse 10), and poisons one-third of the planet's rivers and lakes.

John tells us in verse 11 that "many people died from the waters that had become bitter."

Remember, it isn't going to rain on the earth for 42 months during the reign of the Antichrist. If we think our water bills are high now, just imagine what they would be like if we hadn't had any rain for a few years! Water is going to be an extremely precious commodity.

And now the situation is compounded by another star falling out of heaven and poisoning much of the water that remains.

> The fourth angel sounded his trumpet, and a third of the sun was struck, a third of the moon, and a third of the stars, so that a third of them turned dark. A third of the day was without light, and also a third of the night.
>
> Revelation 8:12

Once again, my mind imagines a heavy meteorite shower falling upon the earth and kicking tons of debris and dust into the upper atmosphere, where it blocks the light from the sun, moon, and stars.

Remember when Mount St. Helens erupted in 1980? A thick cloud of volcanic ash filled the skies over much of the state of Washington, causing darkness at noon.

Just imagine the chaos and terror that will have gripped the earth as these first four judgments have fallen upon it! Fire from heaven will have destroyed much of the forested land and the crops. Much of the sea life will have been killed. The waters and atmosphere will have been polluted.

And now, after all these terrible things, John reports seeing an eagle flying through heaven and crying out:

> "Woe! Woe! Woe to the inhabitants of the earth, because of the trumpet blasts about to be sounded by the other three angels!"   verse 13

Wait a minute! The next three trumpet blasts must *really* be terrible, if this eagle is saying, "Woe to the earth" because of them. It seems as though he'd be saying, "Woe to the earth because of the four trumpets that have already sounded."

Yet it's true. The worst of the judgments are still to come.

> The fifth angel sounded his trumpet, and I saw a star that had fallen from the sky to the earth. The star was given the key to the shaft of the Abyss. When he opened the Abyss, smoke rose from it like the smoke from a gigantic furnace. The sun and sky were darkened by the smoke from the Abyss. And out of the smoke locusts came down upon the earth and were given power like that of scorpions of the earth. They were told not to harm the grass of the earth or any plant or tree, but only those people who did not have the seal of God on their foreheads. They were not given power to kill them, but only to torture them for five months. And the agony they suffered was like that of the sting of a scorpion when it strikes a man. During those days men will seek death, but will not find it; they will long to die, but death will elude them.   Revelation 9:1–6

So we see that as the fifth trumpet is sounded, another star falls from heaven, and this star is given the key to the Abyss, which is also translated as *the bottomless pit.*

Could there really be such a place?

Suppose there was a shaft through the earth's diameter. If someone were to fall into it, he would literally keep on falling forever. He would never hit bottom, but would wind up in the center of the earth, where he would be forever suspended. I believe that such a fissure does exist, and that it leads directly into a place called hell, which lies in the center of the earth.

It is in this pit where the demons are incarcerated. In Luke 8, we read of an incident when Jesus cast a multitude of demons out of a man, and the demons begged Him not to send them into the Abyss before their time.

They knew they would ultimately be consigned to this pit, which is obviously a seething cauldron of unspeakable demonic horror.

Who has been given the keys to this place?

Satan himself, and he is about to unleash all of these demonic forces upon the inhabitants of the earth. This is not the first time in the Bible that Satan is referred to as a star fallen from heaven.

In Isaiah 14:12 we read, "How you have fallen from heaven, O morning star, son of the dawn! You have been cast down to the earth, you who once laid low the nations!" If we continue to read beyond this, we find out just why Lucifer was cast out of heaven in the first place: because he attempted to exalt himself and make himself equal with God. That is a battle he has never given up. And now, as the earth enters its final days, he unleashes all the forces of hell in a final, desperate attack to topple God.

As Satan opens this pit, smoke will billow out of it, further darkening the sky and adding to the stifling, choking pollution that is already troubling mankind.

And out of this choking, stifling smoke will come clouds of demonic hordes that appear as locusts, which have the ability to sting like scorpions. They will possess some form of intelligence, for they are commanded to hurt only those persons who do not have the seal of God on their foreheads. Just what these creatures actually are is not certain—perhaps a mutant form of locust. The fact, in any case, that scientists are now experimenting with gene splicing (and recently performed the first authorized gene transplants into human beings) creates frightening potential.

Locusts can do enough damage even without stingers on their tails. In the history of our nation there have been swarms of locusts that have wiped out entire regions of farmland.

During the 1870s, the skies of Nebraska were darkened by a locust cloud that measured 300 miles long and 100 miles wide. Still, we have not had to suffer through the invasions that some of the Middle Eastern countries have experienced.

I've been told that the locust is a sort of mutation to begin with. Most of the time he's a simple garden-variety grasshopper. But if the climate is dry and food is scarce, he'll go through a Jekyll-and-Hyde transformation and become a monstrous eating machine. His body elongates, his "teeth" sharpen, his appetite is multiplied, and he begins to migrate with other locusts.

Imagine, then, the further transformation of these insects as they develop scorpion-like stingers.

I've never been stung by a scorpion, but I have had a few encounters with bees and wasps. I'm told that a scorpion's sting is much worse than any of these, so it must really be painful! Further, the scorpion native to the Middle East apparently has the worst sting of any variety. At least scorpions don't fly—not now, they don't.

John tells us that this new mutant locust will continue to be an aggressive swarming insect. Only now it won't prey on grass or crops or leaves. Instead, it will go after people, specifically those who do not belong to God.

The world will be tormented by this plague of stinging locusts for five months—and during this time something else very strange is going to happen: Death will take a holiday.

What exactly is death? We don't know. When does it occur? We don't know that, either. That's why we have so many court battles over attempts to turn off equipment that sustains life by "artificial means."

Just the other day I read in the newspaper about a man going to court in an attempt to get his mother's life-support system turned off. His mother, he says, is already dead, even though her heart still beats and her lungs expand and contract.

But while the woman's doctors agree there is no brain activity and relatively no hope of recovery, so long as her body still functions she is considered to be alive, and the hospital will not take responsibility for letting her die.

Is she alive, or is she already dead? Has her spirit left her body, or is it still there? There is no way we can know for sure, and no scientist, philosopher, or theologian can answer that question. We simply don't know when or how the spirit leaves the body.

But imagine what is going to happen when death goes on vacation, and human bodies refuse to die!

For in some cases death is a welcome release. When a person has been suffering, death sets him free from pain to be with God. Just imagine how horrible it would be to suffer such unbearable agony that you would welcome death, and yet know that death will not come.

Imagine a man so tormented that he puts a gun to his head and pulls the trigger—only he does not die. Instead, he continues to walk around with a gaping hole in his head.

We look upon death as an enemy, but I am convinced that this time period when there is no death will be one of the worst in human history. It will be a foretaste of what hell will be like, when the souls of the wicked will be tormented forever without relief and without the possibility of being set free by death.

After five months of this, the terror is over. The locusts disappear as suddenly as they came. Perhaps they have been overcome by a newly developed pesticide, or perhaps they begin to die out naturally. But they are gone and the world begins once again to relax and hope that the worst is over.

It isn't.

Death Returns with a Vengeance

The sixth trumpet is about to be blown, and another slaughter will begin.

John says that an invading army of some 200 million warriors will precipitate a war in which one-third of those still living on the earth will die. For five months death disappeared from the earth, and now it has returned with a vengeance.

When we read verses 13 through 16 of the ninth chapter, we discover that four angels are responsible for all of this destruction. John tells us that these angels were bound at "the great River Euphrates," and that their sole purpose is to kill one-third of all mankind.

Who are these angels? We are not told. Nor are we given to understand what John means by saying that they are "bound" at the Euphrates. But we can know that these angels are in the Middle East today, and that they are involved in bringing God's purposes to pass there: The Euphrates runs right through the heart of Iraq.

No wonder there was so much speculation as to whether or not Saddam Hussein was the Antichrist! Hussein fit many of the characteristics of the Antichrist, but he did not fit them all. Certainly, though, the nation of Iraq is going to be right in the middle of this cataclysmic conflict, as Hussein's unholy legacy lives on.

John goes on to describe the invading army this way:

> The heads of the horses resembled the heads of lions, and out of their mouths came fire, smoke and sulfur. A third of mankind was killed by the three plagues of fire, smoke and sulfur that came out of their mouths. The power of the horses was in their mouths and in their tails; for their tails were like snakes, having heads with which they inflict injury.   Revelation 9:17–19

Not too many years ago those who wanted to discredit the book of Revelation pointed to this particular passage. They found fault with it for two reasons: First, the improbability that any country could field an army of 200 million warriors; second, the belief that all future major wars would be fought by bureaucrats pushing buttons in countries thousands of miles apart from each other, with no conventional forces used.

That's what they used to say. Now we know differently.

Today it is generally acknowledged that Communist China can field a military force of 200 million. (It's not surprising that China should be so militaristic. She was brutalized by the Japanese in World War II, saw millions more die as Communist forces fought for control, and has continuing border skirmishes with her supposed ally, the Soviet Union.)

Will all these 200 million troops come from China? No. Possibly there will also be troops from a confederation of countries. They will be under the generalship of the Antichrist, as he goes about crushing whatever rebellion exists.

And what about the second contention, that all future wars will be fought by remote control?

For an example of how this thinking has changed, review some of the news coverage regarding the 1988 Presidential election campaign between George Bush and Michael Dukakis.

There was a great deal of debate over who would do the better job of beefing up America's conventional forces without increasing our already huge budget deficit. There was much finger-pointing as accusations flew back and forth. Everyone was lamenting the Soviet Union's superior conventional weapons capability, and trying to figure out who was to blame.

A few years back, nobody would have cared much if the Soviets had more tanks than we did. So what? We'll push a few more buttons here and blow those tanks to smithereens.

That sort of thinking has changed. One reason is that smaller nuclear weapons have been developed, weapons that can be fired from tanks and other portable launching systems. This doesn't make war any less destructive; in fact, it adds to the danger.

Who has nuclear weapons? Does Muammar Qadhafi have them in Libya? If he doesn't have them yet, you can bet he's working feverishly to get them, and the thought of a man like that having this destructive potential at his fingertips is frightening.

Think of how many unstable and reactionary governments there are around the world, led by despotic leaders every bit as deranged as Qadhafi who would not hesitate to use nuclear weapons on their enemies.

And there are even more frightening developments.

During World War I, German troops inflicted thousands of casualties by using mustard gas and other chemical weapons. Since then use of these types of weapons—and especially gases that attack the nervous system—has officially been frowned upon by the "civilized" world . . . even as researchers continue to develop stronger and deadlier versions.

Over the last couple of years, we've heard allegations that the Soviet Union has used chemical weapons in Afghanistan. The Russians, of course, have denied it.

Iraq used chemical weapons in its long war with Iran, and also, as I stated earlier, against Kurdish civilians who were seen as disloyal to the regime of Saddam Hussein. More recently on the news, we have seen civilians in Israel and Saudi Arabia wearing their gas masks as they await the arrival of an incoming Scud missile. But there are not enough gas masks for everyone, and if chemical weapons are used on a widespread scale, millions of people will die.

So we have nuclear and chemical weapons proliferating. We have research into weapons utilizing lasers and soundwaves. And we have the ever-increasing destructive power of conventional artillery.

Think about that, and then put yourself in the place of the apostle John, living late in the first century. He is given a vision of millions of soldiers sweeping into battle, using machines and weapons that won't be developed for nearly 2,000 years. John is from an age when armies fought each other with spears and swords; how could he understand bombs, bullets, and chemical warfare? How shocked he would have been to see soldiers carrying rocket launchers, army tanks blasting away with huge artillery shells, and mushroom clouds rising into the sky!

Yet that seems to be what he is describing here:

> A third of mankind was killed by the three plagues of fire, smoke and sulfur.   Revelation 9:18

He talks of "horses" with power in their mouths and in their tails. Could he be referring to tanks with huge gun barrels in front, and smaller artillery to the rear? We can't know for sure what John is describing, but it will involve a war of tremendous proportions. Whoever is involved, and whatever weapons they will be using, millions upon millions of people will be killed.

While all this terror is being unleashed on the earth, those who were raptured before the Tribulation began, and those who were martyred during the Tribulation, will be standing safely before the throne of God, living in joy and peace. Remember, too, that, even during this time of war, God will be making a distinction between the people who belong to Him and those who don't.

How will He be able to keep His people from harm during a time of worldwide destruction? Again, I don't know, but He does, and He will do it.

And now it is almost time for the seventh trumpet blast.

Almost, but not quite. For just as there was a pause between the opening of the first six seals and the seventh, there is also a pause between the sixth and seventh trumpet blasts of the seventh seal.

Preparations must be made before that trumpet blast can sound.

5

The World on the Brink

Revelation 10–11

The world is reeling. War has taken millions of lives. So have a variety of "natural" disasters. There has been famine, fire falling from heaven, and attacks from new, vicious varieties of insects. Now, once again, there is a small break in the action, just as God is about to bring down the final curtain on the earth as we know it.

As we come to the tenth chapter of Revelation, we see that a "mighty angel" has descended from heaven. He is surrounded by a cloud, and has a rainbow over his head, a face that shines like the sun, and feet that flash with fire. He holds in his hand a small scroll as he sets his right foot on the sea, his left foot on the earth, and gives a great shout. Obviously this is no ordinary angel.

As he lifts his right hand to heaven, he swears by Him who lives forever and ever, the Creator of everything that exists, that when the seventh trumpet blast is sounded there will be no more delay, but that God's plan for all mankind will be fulfilled.

Who is this mighty angel? And what does all this mean?

Although some will disagree with me, I believe that this is none other than Jesus Christ, and that the scroll He is holding is the title deed for the earth. Now that the seals have been broken, the scroll has been opened, showing that ownership of the earth has reverted to the rightful owner—God Himself.

There are several reasons to believe that this "angel" is actually Christ. For one thing, only Christ was worthy of opening the scroll, and this being holds it in his hand. For another, He is descending on a cloud, which is exactly how Jesus will return to the earth (Luke 21:27).

Finally, He gives a triumphant shout of victory, which is likened to the roar of a lion. The Old Testament contains several references to the Lord shouting or roaring like a lion. Jeremiah 25:30 says that He will "roar" from on high. And in Hosea 11:10 the Lord says, speaking through His prophet, that He will "roar like a lion." Once again, in Joel 3:16, the Lord is described as roaring and thundering as the earth and sky begin to shake.

As I said, not everyone agrees with me that this is Jesus Christ, and some argue the point on the basis of this "angel" swearing by Him who lives forever and ever. Why, they ask, would God appeal to God as a higher authority?

Because there is no higher authority than God. He can do no better than to swear by Himself.

Whenever a man goes to court he is asked to put his hand on the Bible and swear that he is going to tell the truth. He is even asked to add the words *So help me, God.* Our society recognizes that there is no higher authority than God and His Word.

If you want to establish the credibility of what you are going to say, you swear on something higher than yourself. No one would pay attention if you swore on the Yellow Pages or the Sears and Roebuck catalog.

The writer of Hebrews tells us that when God made a promise to Abraham, He swore by His own name, because there was no one greater to swear by (7:21). So I do not find it at all inconsistent that Jesus Christ, being equal with God, would swear by God.

God's Timing Is Perfect

When Jesus roars out His cry of triumph, John hears the voices of seven thunders crashing in reply. But as he begins to write down what the thunders have said, a voice from heaven commands him not to do it. These secrets are not yet to be revealed.

Why doesn't God want us to know? Is He hiding something from us? No, He will tell us everything as we need to know it, or as we're capable of handling it. But as far as what the thunders have said, that time has not yet come.

I am reminded of Jesus' words at the Last Supper, as recorded in John 16:12. Explaining to His disciples all that was about to happen to Him, He said He had much more He wanted to tell them, but He couldn't because they were not able to "bear" it.

As we read that passage, we sense the agony and urgency in Jesus' heart. He didn't want to keep anything back from these men who had become His dearest friends, yet He knew there was no way they could comprehend the deepest secrets of the heart of God.

This may be the case with the secrets of the seven thunders. When we are ready to understand, we will be told, but not until then.

This mystery of God's timing applies to all areas of our lives. Have you ever grown impatient waiting for God to do something? I know I have. Some nights I look up at a big, luminous moon hanging in the sky, and my heart swells with worship. I feel I just can't wait another day for the Rapture to come. "Lord, when are You going to take Your people home?"

Then there are times when I'm impatient regarding less significant matters, like wanting to know God's direction in a particular situation. I've prayed for guidance, but none comes. God knows what I should do, but He's not telling me.

"God, what's the problem? I want Your guidance and I want it now!"

One thing we all have to learn is that God's timing is perfect.

Everyone has seen TV commercials for the company that promises not to sell any of its wine "before its time." I'm certain that commercial has sold gallons and gallons of wine, though I'm not sure what the slogan really means. But what may be just a good slogan for a wine bottler is an excellent description of the way God works. He will do nothing out of its proper time.

When will the Rapture occur? I don't know for sure, but I know that the timing will be absolutely perfect!

What about the start of the Tribulation? Again, the only thing I can say for certain is that the timing will be exactly right.

Sometimes it's hard to be patient, especially when we need God to move in certain ways and we can't understand why He's not doing it. But no matter what our emotions tell us, no matter what the world says, God's timing is always perfect— He's never early, He's never late. Do yourself a favor—try to stay in step with Him. Don't run ahead, tempting Him by doing things He hasn't told you to do; and don't straggle behind disobediently.

Have you ever wondered why one ministry succeeds and another fails? Both are staffed by competent people. Both follow the same pattern of development. But one collapses after only a few months, and the other operates for years. Why? In most cases, those involved with the ministry that succeeded spent time seeking God and attempting to follow His timing, whereas the others just took a giant step in the dark and expected Him to bless after the fact.

"God, what's wrong?" they pray as they see their efforts crumbling. "We're doing this for You. Why aren't You blessing us?"

"I never told you to start this ministry," God says. "You didn't listen to Me, and your timing was not My timing."

There are many people who don't believe that this world will ever stop turning: "Oh, it may happen a billion years or so from now, but it's certainly not going to happen within my lifetime. You can talk all you want about how these are the last days, but I just don't believe it. Every day's the same—the sun goes up, the sun goes down, the sun comes back up again. It's been that way for millions of years. Why should I believe it's going to change?"

What they don't understand is that God has not delayed fulfilling His plan for any other reason except that His timing is always perfect. When this planet has been through everything God has designed for it, then and only then will God's final plan begin to unfold. God knows how many souls will be brought into the Kingdom. He knows the names of babies who have yet to be born. He is leaving nothing—absolutely nothing—to chance. We can't hurry Him into action until all is ready. And when it is, there is nothing we can do to hold back His hand.

So now we have Jesus Christ standing on the earth, holding the title deed to the planet. He has told us that the delay is over, and that God's plan for the earth is about to be fulfilled. And a very strange thing happens.

> Then the voice that I had heard from heaven spoke to me once more: "Go, take the scroll that lies open in the hand of the angel who is standing on the sea and on the land."
>
> So I went to the angel and asked him to give me the little scroll. He said to me, "Take it and eat it. It will turn your stomach sour, but in your mouth it will be as sweet as honey." I took the little scroll from the angel's hand and ate it. It tasted as sweet as honey in my mouth, but when I had eaten it, my stomach turned sour.
>
> Revelation 10:8–10

At this point some people throw up their hands in dismay. "Okay, John, you've completely lost me now. Why in the world would you want to eat the title deed to the earth?"

It's really not as hard to understand as it might seem at first glance.

In this instance, John is devouring the scroll, which contains the words of God. You've undoubtedly heard of someone "devouring" a good book, which means they're hanging onto every word. That is what John is being told to do as he hears and witnesses God's plans for the earth.

It's as if God is saying, "Pay very close attention, John, because everything you are going to see is extremely important."

Why does the scroll taste sweet and then turn bitter in the apostle's stomach?

The sweet taste represents the hope of the earth's bright future when God's Kingdom has been established. This will be the time spoken of by the Old Testament prophets, when the lion will lie down with the lamb and there will be nothing but peace, joy, and harmony from pole to pole.

But the bitterness represents what will take place upon the earth *before* God's Kingdom can be established—the terrible judgments we have already read about, and other disasters that are still to come. You might say that hearing about the trouble that is to come upon the earth is a bitter pill for John to swallow.

Nevertheless, John now has these words of God within him, and he is told that he must once again begin prophesying about things that will happen to many peoples, nations, languages, and kings.

Reconstruction of the Temple

But before he begins to prophesy, he is told to take a measuring rod and to "go and measure the temple of God and the altar, and count the worshipers there" (Revelation 11:1).

What temple is John talking about? Well, I guarantee you

that it's not the Mormon Temple in Salt Lake City or a Buddhist temple in Bangkok. It's the Temple of God in Jerusalem—the city He has chosen for His capital.

John would be in trouble if he went to Jerusalem today to measure the Temple because it isn't there. It was destroyed many centuries ago, just as Jesus predicted (Matthew 24:2). John could measure el-Aqsa Mosque or the Dome of the Rock. But that's not what he was commanded to do.

No, the order is specific: "Go and measure the temple of God."

This can mean only one thing, and that's that the Temple will be rebuilt in Jerusalem. Every so often I come across a newspaper or magazine article about some plan to rebuild the Temple. Whenever I do, I get a little shiver down my spine, because I know that construction of the Temple will take place during the Tribulation. Every sign that construction of the Temple is closer is also a sign that the Tribulation, and thus the Rapture, is closer, too.

The Bible gives several signs to look for as an indication that the end of the age is almost here. One of the strongest is that the Jewish people, who have been scattered all over the earth, will be brought back home to Israel. The twentieth century has seen that happen, and it truly is a remarkable thing.

Just 75 years ago there appeared to be little chance that there would ever again be a Jewish homeland. The Jewish people had been scattered to the four winds, and it's a miracle that they were able to retain their identity as Jews while inhabiting almost every nation on earth. But then God began to move, fulfilling promises He had made thousands of years before, and Jews by the thousands began returning to the Middle East.

In 1948, establishment of the state of Israel officially fulfilled the prophecy of the regathering of God's people. This is especially significant when we consider the words of Jesus as recorded in Luke 21:24: "Jerusalem will be trampled on by the Gentiles until the times of the Gentiles are fulfilled." He then goes on to explain that the fulfilling of these "times of the Gentiles" will also mean the approach of the end of that age.

At the present time, a small but dedicated group of Jewish people is trying to clear the way to rebuild the Temple. In fact, there are at least two organizations in Jerusalem that have pledged themselves to the sole purpose of seeing the Temple rebuilt.

Some of these people are extremely radical. They advocate using force to run the Muslims out of the area and destroying the Dome of the Rock so that the Temple may be rebuilt on the site where it now stands. Within the last couple of years, several Israeli extremists were arrested and charged because of their involvement in a plot to blow up the Dome of the Rock. But they didn't know there's nothing they can do until after the Rapture. As soon as the Christians are out of here, then it's in their hands!

There are others who hold a more moderate view, believing that the Temple Mount should be divided so as not to create a holy war between Muslims and Jews. This group would build a wall just to the north side of the Dome of the Rock and construct the Temple on the northern side of the wall.

Dr. Asher Kaufman is a scholar who has made an extensive study of the Temple Mount. While the results of Dr. Kaufman's study remain controversial among biblical archaeologists, his research into ancient records has led him to believe that the Temple as it was originally built by King Solomon actually stood to the north of the present-day Dome of the Rock.

He has even pinpointed a spot, 322 feet north of the Dome of the Rock, where the Holy of Holies was located in Solomon's Temple.

I also believe that Jewish believers will gather in the Temple to worship God in the same ways their ancestors did thousands of years ago. (There is even a *yeshiva* within the walled city of Jerusalem where students are being taught how to butcher animals for sacrifice to God according to the laws of Moses.)

Yes, I believe that the Dome of the Rock will share the Temple Mount with the rebuilt Temple. This makes sense, especially when we consider the words of Revelation 11:2. For when John was told to measure the new Temple and the courts, he was commanded:

> "Exclude the outer court; do not measure it, because it has been given to the Gentiles."

I believe this is a reference to the Dome of the Rock, which sits on property that was once part of the outer court of the Temple of Solomon, according to Dr. Kaufman's research.

In the book of Ezekiel we see another prophecy about the Temple that is to be rebuilt in Jerusalem. Ezekiel, like John, is told to measure it.

Ezekiel recounts that he measured a wall that was around the Temple, and that the wall had the purpose of separating the holy place from the profane (Ezekiel 42:20).

The holy place, of course, would be the Temple. And I believe the profane is the Dome of the Rock.

There is some debate as to when the Temple will be rebuilt. I believe construction will be completed during the Tribulation, and specifically during the reign of the Antichrist. That's because I also believe the Antichrist will arrive on the world's stage as a champion of the people. He'll strive to be seen as a man of peace and love who tolerates all religions—and even supports them.

Is the Antichrist going to come out of the Soviet Union? I really don't think so, because the Communists are very up-front with their feelings about religion. They may want to be seen as tolerant, but they will not likely do anything to encourage religion of any sort.

When the Antichrist comes, on the other hand, he will do everything within his power to keep his true views from becoming known—at first.

And so he will make a covenant with Israel according to the prophecy of Daniel 9, giving them the go-ahead to rebuild the Temple in Jerusalem. Furthermore, I believe he will be hailed as a remarkable statesman for his ability to get the Muslims to give their backing to the rebuilding of the Temple.

Everything will be peace, love, and harmony, and if there are any aging hippies left around, they'll think the age of Aquarius has finally arrived. But they'll be wrong again, just as they were in the 1960s!

For halfway into his seven-year reign, the Antichrist will break his pact with the Jewish people, take up residence in the Temple, and declare that he should be worshiped as God almighty. (See 2 Thessalonians 2.)

And so for the next 42 months, the holy city of Jerusalem will once again be trampled on by the Gentiles.

The Return of Elijah

"And I will give power to my two witnesses, and they will prophesy for 1,260 days, clothed in sackcloth." These are the two olive trees and the two lampstands that stand before the Lord of the earth. If anyone tries to harm them, fire comes from their mouths and devours their enemies. This is how anyone who wants to harm them must die.

Revelation 11:3–5

As soon as the Tribulation period has begun, God says that He will send His two witnesses to Jerusalem to preach to His chosen people, the Jews.

What does John mean when he tells us that these witnesses are the two olive trees and the two lampstands that stand before the Lord of the earth?

John is talking about events that were also prophesied by the prophet Zechariah. In the fourth chapter of his book, Zechariah talks about these same two olive trees, writing in verses 11–14:

> Then I asked the angel, "What are these two olive trees
> on the right and the left of the lampstand?"
>
> Again I asked him, "What are these two olive branches
> beside the two gold pipes that pour out golden oil?"
>
> He replied, "Do you not know what these are?"
>
> "No, my Lord," I said.
>
> So he said, "These are the two who are anointed to serve
> the Lord of all the earth."

Far from being obscure and symbolic, John is actually explaining the vision Zechariah beheld several hundred years previously.

When the two witnesses arrive on the scene, their presence will also fulfill the prophecy found in the last two verses of the Old Testament. In Malachi 4:5–6, we read:

> "See, I will send you the prophet Elijah before that great
> and dreadful day of the Lord comes. He will turn the
> hearts of the fathers to their children, and the hearts of the
> children to their fathers; or else I will come and strike the
> land with a curse."

One of these two witnesses will be the prophet Elijah returned to the earth.

He has long been expected by the Jewish people. When John the Baptist was preaching in the wilderness, some people came to ask if he were Elijah (John 1:21). And when Jesus asked His disciples what people were saying about Him, they told Him that some people thought He was Elijah (Matthew 16:13–14).

But at that time the coming of Elijah was still far in the future.

Another reason we can say that one of these two witnesses will be Elijah himself is that John tells us fire will go out from the witnesses to destroy anyone who attempts to harm them.

Since this is the case, it seems that Elijah will be up to his old tricks.

Remember what happened when King Ahaziah sent his soldiers to arrest Elijah because he didn't like Elijah's prophecy (2 Kings 1:1–15)? The first captain came with fifty men and demanded that Elijah surrender to them. Instead, fire came down from heaven and consumed the whole company. Undaunted, the king sent another captain, with another fifty men, but the same thing happened.

The king must have been beside himself with anger as he sent out a third company. He was undoubtedly thinking, *What kind of army do I have that one man can do this to them?*

Imagine how that third captain must have felt as he approached Elijah and saw nothing but charred ashes where his comrades-in-arms once stood. Deciding he had better try a different tactic, he got down on his knees and humbly asked the prophet to go with him.

At this point, Elijah surrendered and went along peacefully. He knew that this captain respected him as God's prophet, and also respected the word of the Lord.

Elijah apparently won't have changed much when he appears in the end times, because John says that those who seek to harm him will suffer the same fate as Ahaziah's soldiers.

I have been asked from time to time who I believe the other witness will be. I don't know, but I presume it will be another of the great men of the Old Testament. Some believe it will be Moses, which makes sense because Moses and Elijah appeared together and talked with Jesus on the Mount of Transfiguration (see Mark 9:4). Since they have worked together before, it's logical to assume that they might work together again.

Whereas Elijah never died, moreover, but was taken from the earth in a fiery chariot, the death of Moses was surrounded by what we might call "mysterious" circumstances. In Deuteronomy 34:5–6, we read: "And Moses the servant of the Lord died there in Moab, as the Lord had said. He buried him in Moab, in the valley opposite Beth Peor, but to this day no one knows where his grave is."

The book of Jude also tells us that the devil and the archangel Michael had some sort of dispute over the body of Moses (verse 9). Why? What was so special about Moses' body? Could it be that the devil knew Moses would be returning to the earth in the last days, and sought to prevent it from happening?

I also wonder why God chose to bury Moses. There have been many other great men and women of God whom He has never chosen to bury—not even Jesus, who was taken from His cross by friends and placed in a manmade tomb prior to the resurrection.

Inasmuch as they are called the two witnesses, how appropriate it would be for Moses and Elijah to be selected, since the Old Testament is often referred to as "the Law and the prophets." Moses represents the Law and Elijah the prophets. So I'd say that those who speculate that one of the witnesses will be Moses do so on pretty good authority.

Others, though, are just as convincing in their argument that the other witness will be Enoch, who "walked with God; then he was no more, because God took him away" (Genesis 5:24).

Of all the great men and women of history—excluding those who are alive today—there are only two who never tasted death. One was Elijah and the other was Enoch. All the great kings and queens, philosophers, and scientists have ultimately had to face death. Why not Elijah? Why not Enoch? Could it be that God knew their work was not finished?

We know that eventually the two witnesses will be killed, and so it could be that these two mighty men of God are coming back to face the deaths from which God allowed them to escape many hundreds of years ago.

The Bible teaches that "man is destined to die once, and after that to face judgment" (Hebrews 9:27). Or, as it says in the King James Version, "It is appointed unto men once to die." And so it could be that Elijah and Enoch are coming back not only to serve as witnesses for God, but to keep their own appointments with death.

These two men are going to be powerful indeed. John tells us that they will be able to bring plagues upon the earth, and, as I've mentioned before, they will use their power to keep it from raining on the earth for 42 months. You probably remember that Elijah prayed during the reign of evil King Ahab, and it didn't rain in Israel for three years (1 Kings 17:1–18:1). Once again history will repeat itself when Elijah returns to the earth.

We can imagine how much the world will fear and hate these men. "If only we could get rid of these two guys, everything would be fine!" people will say, not realizing that their own unbelief and sins are causing these calamities to come upon them. Many *will* listen to what these two witnesses say and will turn their lives over to God, but many more will choose to regard these two as evil and will plot to destroy them.

No matter how hard they try, however, no one will be able to touch the two witnesses until they have completed the work God has called them to do.

Have you ever had a close call with death or serious injury and wondered later how you managed to escape? Have there been occasions when you've fallen onto your knees to thank the Lord for His protection?

I talked with an evangelist friend recently who had just had one of those experiences. He was driving home, exhausted, after conducting an evangelistic crusade. When the white line down the middle of the road began to get blurry, he decided to pull off to the side for a quick nap. Sure enough, after about fifteen minutes he was feeling much better and decided to resume his trip.

Pulling up to the edge of the highway, he looked to make sure there was no traffic coming. Not seeing anything, he prepared to step on the accelerator and pull out onto the road. But as he started to push down on the pedal he hesitated for just a couple of seconds. As he did, he felt a powerful rush of wind, as a huge tractor-trailer rig sped by.

"Where that truck came from I'll never know," he told me. "I suppose that because I was so tired I just didn't see him coming. And I'll never know what made me hesitate before stepping on the gas, either. Well, actually, yes, I do know—it was nothing but the grace of God."

Had God not intervened in that situation, the evangelist would have pulled into the path of the truck and been killed. But God isn't finished with him yet: That evangelist still has things to accomplish on the earth.

The truth is, God will give us His divine protection until we have accomplished that for which we have been put upon the earth. I believe that every man, woman, and child is here for a specific purpose, and that God will give us every opportunity we need to find and fulfill it.

God's Prophets Defeated

So the two witnesses will be spared from all attempts on their lives until they have fulfilled their calling, which is to witness in Jerusalem for 1,260 days. After this time, God will allow the powers of hell to come against them, and they will be killed.

> Now when they have finished their testimony, the beast that comes up from the Abyss will attack them, and overpower and kill them. Their bodies will lie in the street of the great city, which is figuratively called Sodom and Egypt, where also their Lord was crucified. For three and a half days men from every people, tribe, language and nation will gaze on their bodies and refuse them burial. The inhabitants of the earth will gloat over them and will

celebrate by sending each other gifts, because these two
prophets had tormented those who live on the earth.

Revelation 11:7–10

The witnesses' deaths will cause a time of rejoicing and celebration all over the earth. John says that people will be so glad
to get rid of them that they'll celebrate by sending each other
gifts! They'll relax once again, thinking, "Now that we've gotten rid of those two, we can get back to life as usual."

Before we see what happens next, consider the words of John
when he tells us that the corpses of the witnesses will lie in the
streets of Jerusalem for more than three days while "men from
every people, tribe, language and nation will gaze on their
bodies."

Prior to the last 25 years, there was no way this could have
taken place. But with the advent of broadcasting by satellite, it
has become commonplace to sit in our living rooms in the
United States and watch something being transmitted live from
halfway around the world. And so news crews from all the
major television networks will converge on Jerusalem in order
to send back live reports.

I can just imagine reporters and photographers from ABC,
CBS, NBC, and CNN fighting for the best positions, each trying to grab the best angle on the story.

We can see how hated these two men will have become when
we read that people will allow their bodies to lie in the streets
for three days without giving them a decent burial. It reminds
me of photographs I've seen of Benito Mussolini's body being
displayed in Milan near the end of World War II. (The difference, of course, is that Mussolini had misruled Italy and led her
into a destructive and costly war, whereas the two witnesses
have merely insisted that people repent and turn back to God.)

When I think about what's going to happen, I can see people
sitting in front of their TV sets, nibbling on chips and dip,
gulping down cans of beer and soda, listening to the Antichrist

tell them that the danger is past and that his forces have made the world safe once again.

But these millions of TV viewers are in for a surprise of colossal proportions, because on the fourth day after their deaths, the two witnesses will come back to life. With all those TV cameras and klieg lights still trained on them, they'll suddenly rise to their feet as "a breath of life from God" enters into them (Revelation 11:11).

Can you just imagine it?

"Ladies and gentlemen, we interrupt 'The Cosby Show' to take you live to Jerusalem for a special news report."

Then a frantic-faced reporter will come onto the screen, explaining breathlessly how a most amazing thing has just happened. The two "rebels" who had been presumed dead have apparently recovered from their wounds and are back on their feet.

He will go to a live picture of the two witnesses walking through the streets of Jerusalem, and then the whole world will see them ascend into the air, as God calls them home to heaven.

Immediately all the networks will find their phone lines jammed with calls from people wanting to know what's really happening. Is it for real, they'll ask, or simply some crazy hoax or even a new special effects technique?

As for the Antichrist, he'll have a big public relations job on his hands. How can he come out of this looking good, convincing people to believe that the witnesses were just a couple of dangerous, crazy terrorists?

He won't have much time to spend on strategy, though, because almost as soon as the witnesses rise into the sky, Jerusalem will suffer a devastating earthquake. Fully one-tenth of the city will be destroyed, and some seven thousand people will be killed (verse 13).

John tells us that the terrified survivors will finally begin to give glory to God, recognizing at last that He is in charge of all that is going on upon the earth.

The Seventh Trumpet Sounds

Do you remember that the scroll representing the title deed to the earth was bound with seven seals? As those seals were opened, various judgments were poured out upon the earth. Then, as the final seal was opened, seven angels appeared on the scene, each holding a trumpet to blow. As those trumpet blasts were sounded, more of God's judgments fell upon the earth. We were just about to hear the seventh angel sound his trumpet when the two witnesses arrived on the scene.

Now that these men of God have been killed and resurrected, and Jerusalem has been hit hard with the ensuing earthquake, the angel puts the trumpet to his lips and sounds a loud blast.

John tells us that this is followed by loud voices in heaven that proclaim:

> "The kingdom of the world has become the kingdom of
> our Lord and of his Christ, and he will reign for ever and
> ever."   Revelation 11–15

If anyone looks around at what is happening on the earth at this time, he will not think that God is in control. The Antichrist will still be firmly in power, despite the fact that these two witnesses and the earthquake in Jerusalem have given him a whale of a public relations headache. There will be many believers on the planet, but they will be vastly outnumbered by those who pledge their support to the Antichrist.

As far as the earth itself is concerned, it will still be reeling under the onslaught of the long string of natural disasters we have already mentioned.

The voices proclaim that the kingdom of the world has become the Kingdom of the Lord, but anyone taking a casual glance around the planet would have to say that it must still be held very tightly in Satan's grip. And yet the seals on the scrolls will have been broken, and the world will have returned to its rightful owner.

The victory has already been won, even if the evidence is not apparent.

John tells us that the elders who are before the throne of God in heaven will recognize this, too, and fall down before Him in worship. They'll thank Him because He has chosen this as the time to reward those who have been faithful to Him, and to destroy those who have opposed Him.

As their celebration continues, John says that the Temple of God will open in heaven, and the Ark of His covenant will be seen.

Meanwhile, all around the earth, lightning will flash, thunder will crash, hail will fall, and there will be a great earthquake.

God is about to move in a mighty way.

6

The Woman, the Dragon, and the Creature from the Sea

Revelation 12–13

When people think about the book of Revelation, they usually recall some of the strange creatures that populate the book: The dragon, the creature from the sea, the woman who wears stars for a crown.

Who are these beings? And what do they have to do with us?

As we come to the twelfth chapter of Revelation, we're about to find out.

> A great and wondrous sign appeared in heaven: a woman clothed with the sun, with the moon under her feet and a crown of twelve stars on her head. She was pregnant and cried out in pain as she was about to give birth. Then another sign appeared in heaven: an enormous red dragon with seven heads and ten horns and seven crowns on his heads. His tail swept a third of the stars out of the sky and flung them to the earth. The dragon stood in front of the woman who was about to give birth, so that he might devour her child the moment it was born. She gave birth to a son, a male child, who will rule all the nations with an iron scepter. And her child was snatched up to God and to his throne. The woman fled into the desert to a place prepared for her by God, where she might be taken care of for 1,260 days. Revelation 12:1–6

First, who is this woman? We can get the answer by turning to Genesis 37:9–11 and reading the account of one of Joseph's dreams. In it eleven stars, plus the sun and moon, bowed down before him.

The eleven stars represented his brothers, while the sun was his father, Jacob, and the moon was his mother, Rachel. You may remember that his brothers were unhappy—understandably so, perhaps—when he told them of his dream. But however they felt about it, it did come true years later when Joseph rose to great power in Egypt.

Jacob, you will also remember, was the grandson of Abraham, who is the father of the Jewish people. God changed Jacob's name to Israel, and his sons—Joseph and his brothers— were the fathers of the twelve tribes of Israel.

The stars in this woman's crown, therefore, represent the tribes of Israel—just as the stars did in Joseph's dream; and the woman in labor represents the nation of Israel.

But who is her child? And why does this terrible dragon want to destroy him?

Throughout the Old Testament, we read that the Jews are God's "chosen people." But why did He choose them? For one purpose, and that was to be the people who would bring the Messiah—His Son, Jesus Christ—into the world. God promised Abraham that "all peoples on earth will be blessed through you" (Genesis 12:3), and He did this by bringing the Savior of the world through Abraham's line.

The Messiah was to be a direct descendant of Abraham and David, two of the greatest leaders the Hebrew race has ever produced. And so God gave the Jewish people His laws. He blessed them with His promises. He gave them the favor of His presence.

Tragically, when the Messiah was born, the One for whom the Jews had been waiting all those thousands of years, most of them turned away from Him.

So, whereas the woman represents the nation of Israel about to give birth to the Messiah, the dragon is Satan, who will do anything he can to keep the Messiah from accomplishing His mission.

Satan has always looked for ways to thwart God's plan of redemption. Remember, when Christ was born, that wise men came to Herod, asking if he knew where the new king might be. It was a natural mistake for the wise men to make, for surely any newborn king would be the son of the existing king—in this case, Herod.

Herod told them he didn't know, but asked them to come back when they found the child. He said he wanted to go see the baby for himself, to pay his respects.

Of course, Herod had no intention of doing anything but eliminating his rival. He figured this country wasn't big enough for two kings, and he planned to hold onto his position. If the wise men had come back to his palace and told him where the Baby Jesus was, he would have killed the holy Infant. Fortunately, the wise men were directed by God not to return to Herod with this important information (Matthew 2:12).

Not one for taking chances, Herod decided to slaughter every child under two years of age within the area of Bethlehem, thus ensuring the elimination of his competition. Who cared if he had to kill a few hundred innocent children along the way?

But once again Herod's plans—and therefore, Satan's plans—were foiled when an angel warned Joseph in a dream to take his wife, Mary, and the Baby Jesus and flee into Egypt, where they would be safe from Herod's anger.

Satan was like a dragon waiting to pounce on the Messiah as soon as He came into the world. But Satan's cunning, though it caused pain and anguish, was no match for God. It never has been and it never will be.

Satan wasn't through, of course. He tried again to defeat Jesus when he met Him in the wilderness and sought to tempt

Him into sinning. And he unleashed his full fury when Jesus was condemned in an unfair trail and crucified on trumped-up charges. But even then, the old dragon's greatest victory turned into his greatest defeat when Jesus walked out of the tomb on the third day after His death.

After His resurrection He ascended into heaven, just as the infant in John's vision was caught up into heaven. That's where Jesus is right now, sitting at the right hand of the Father, waiting for all things to be brought into subjection to Him, and for the day when He will return to the earth in glory and power.

The Ancient Rebellion

What about the stars that are swept from heaven by the dragon's tail? This is an obvious reference to Satan's fall from heaven.

I'm sure you know that many theologians believe that before he rebelled against God, Satan was an archangel, one of the most important angels in all of heaven (Ezekiel 28:12–19).

There were perhaps three of these angels: Gabriel, Michael, and Lucifer. It may be assumed that each of them acted as a governor or prince, with one-third of the other angels under his authority. And it is believed that when Satan—or Lucifer— rebelled against God, most or perhaps all of the angels under his authority joined him. John's vision would also seem to indicate this.

We don't know when the rebellion occurred, or why, although many Scriptures refer to Satan's pride, and to his desire to be equal with God. (See Isaiah 14:11–15, for example.)

This heavenly civil war undoubtedly occurred sometime before the creation of man, and it has been suggested that Satan rebelled because he was opposed to God's plan to create man in the first place. That would seem to make sense, because ever since Adam was created Satan has been doing everything within his power to prove that man was nothing more than a colossal mistake.

In the first chapter of the book of Job, we are told that Satan came before God's throne and insisted that Job was faithful to the Lord only because of all the blessings in his life (Job 1:10–11).

Satan said, in effect, "If you take all those blessings away from him, he'll turn against You, just like that."

Job wasn't alone in being on trial; we all are, because Satan is our accuser. He wants us to disappoint God, and he'll do anything to accomplish his purpose. He's always probing, looking for a weakness, and once he's found it, will keep pounding away at that spot with all his might.

Happily, Job did not turn against God, even though he lost all his riches, most of his family, and was afflicted with a painful disease. How disappointed Satan must have been to be proved wrong once again!

We see, then, that these first two parts of John's vision have to do with the past—the birth of Christ and the rebellion of Satan. We come now to events that will take place in the future.

First of all, the woman who has given birth flees into the wilderness.

Jesus warned His disciples about this in Matthew 24:15–21:

> "So when you see standing in the holy place 'the abomination that causes desolation,' spoken of through the prophet Daniel—let the reader understand—then let those who are in Judea flee to the mountains. Let no one on the roof of his house go down to take anything out of the house. Let no one in the field go back to get his cloak. How dreadful it will be in those days for pregnant women and nursing mothers! Pray that your flight will not take place in winter or on the Sabbath. For then there will be

great distress, unequaled from the beginning of the world
until now—and never to be equaled again."

"The abomination that causes desolation": what was Jesus
talking about?

He was referring to the time when the Antichrist will come
to Jerusalem and enter the Temple—not only the Temple, in
fact, but the most sacred part of the Temple, the Holy of
Holies—and take up his residence there. He will, for the first
time, proclaim that he is much more than a popular political
leader. He will claim to be God incarnate, and he will expect
to be worshiped as such (2 Thessalonians 2:4; Daniel 9:27).

Surprisingly, the Antichrist's proclamation will be accepted
by many people around the world. They will look at the way
he brought the world together under his banner and decide that
he could have done so only through supernatural means. They
will be right, but they won't realize that there are two supernatural forces at work in the universe. Not everything supernatural
is of God.

Some of those who accept the Antichrist's proclamation of
himself as God will not really believe him, because they won't
believe in any sort of god. They will be atheists who will say,
"He makes as good a god as any," or, "If he wants to think he's
God, that's fine, just as long as he keeps the world in peace."

But you won't find very many people with that attitude in the
nation of Israel.

The Antichrist's action will precipitate a spiritual revival of
unprecedented proportions within that nation. It will also precipitate a bloody rebellion.

Millions of Jews throughout Israel and the rest of the world
will awaken to their spiritual heritage. They will see that they
must either serve God or the Antichrist. There are no other
options.

Neutrality will not be tolerated by the Antichrist. Those who refuse to worship him as God will be persecuted relentlessly.

In order to escape persecution, many Jews will flee into the wilderness outside of Jerusalem. It is likely that many of them will take refuge in the rock city of Petra, which sits to the south and east of the Dead Sea, in the Ha'arva valley in Jordan. Petra is an impregnable fortress, and God will watch over them there for three years, just as he watched over the children of Israel for forty years in the wilderness.

And now John's vision reveals a great battle in heaven, pitting Michael and his angels against the dragon and his angels. Michael prevails and the dragon and his angels are cast down to the earth.

At this point, John hears a loud voice in heaven:

> "Now have come the salvation and the power and the
> kingdom of our God, and the authority of his Christ. For
> the accuser of our brothers, who accuses them before our
> God day and night, has been hurled down."
>
> Revelation 12:10

In essence God has said to Satan, "I'm tired of hearing you bad-mouthing My people, and I'm not going to put up with it any longer."

Up until this point, Satan has apparently had access to heaven. He has been able to come and go as he pleases, relishing his role as the badgering prosecuting attorney.

Over the last couple of years, courtroom TV dramas have become extremely popular. We have "People's Court," "Divorce Court," "Superior Court," "The Judge," and a plethora of similar shows. I believe part of the reason these shows have succeeded is that people love to see a tough attorney cross-examining someone:

"You weren't really at home the night of August 14, were you, Mr. Ferguson?"

"Yes, yes, of course I was."

"No, you weren't, Mr. Ferguson. In fact, you were riding your motorcycle down Fremont Street looking for a fight, weren't you?"

"No, I'm innocent, I tell you!"

But no matter how much poor Mr. Ferguson protests his innocence, the prosecuting attorney will not ease up.

That's how Satan acts toward us. He never gets tired of finding our faults, of pointing them out to God, of charging that we're worthless and faithless, just as he said about Job.

Satan can carry on all he wants when it comes to those of us who have accepted Jesus Christ as Lord and Savior, because God looks at us and says, "Satan, I don't know what you're talking about! They are clothed in My Son's holiness and righteousness."

This makes Satan furious because he knows very well how far from holiness and righteousness we really are. But the righteousness of Christ covers us, and that's all the Father sees when He looks our way.

Not only have Michael and his angels overcome Satan; the voice tells John that those who have remained faithful to God in spite of terrible persecution have also contributed to his downfall!

> "They overcame him by the blood of the Lamb and by the word of their testimony; they did not love their lives so much as to shrink from death."   verse 11

Satan Is Furious

The fact that Satan has been barred from heaven once and for all is great news to the people of God, but not to the earth as a whole.

"Woe to the earth and the sea, because the devil has gone
down to you! He is filled with fury, because he knows that
his time is short."   verse 12

No sooner does Satan land on the earth than he takes off in
hot pursuit of the woman (Israel) who gave birth to the male
child. He chases her, but she sprouts wings so that she might
fly to her place of refuge in the desert, where she will be taken
care of for "a time, times and half a time." (See also Daniel
12:7.) Because a "time" is generally considered to be equal to
a year, we may assume that these Jewish believers will be protected for the final three-and-a-half year period (one time plus
two times plus one-half a time) of the Antichrist's rule and the
Tribulation.

John explains further:

> Then from his mouth the serpent spewed water like a
> river, to overtake the woman and sweep her away with the
> torrent. But the earth helped the woman by opening its
> mouth and swallowing the river that the dragon had
> spewed out of his mouth. Then the dragon was enraged at
> the woman and went off to make war against the rest of
> her offspring—those who obey God's commandments and
> hold to the testimony of Jesus.   Revelation 12:15–17

During these last days of the planet's existence, Satan will
pursue his ultimate goal of toppling God by doing everything
he can to destroy the Jewish people. But he will not be able to
prevail.

Have you ever wondered why Adolf Hitler murdered some
six million innocent Jews? Was he just a raving lunatic who
needed someone to pick on and decided on the Jewish people
as his target? If Hitler were simply crazy, why did he have so
many military successes? How was he able to win the minds of
a whole nation, so that one of the most cultured countries on

earth turned into a gigantic, savage, hate-filled prison?

No, Hitler was not some lone lunatic acting on his own who just managed somehow to climb the ladder of political power. He was completely in the grip of the devil. He had Satan's wisdom in his mind and Satan's hatred in his soul. He declared that the Jews were troublemakers, a blight on society, the ones who hoarded material goods while others went hungry and did without.

Many of the German people believed the devious lies Hitler told them, and he may have even believed them himself. But beneath it all, Hitler's war against the Jews was an attempt to wipe God's chosen people off the face of the earth.

When you stop to think about it, it is amazing that the Jewish people survived. Hitler butchered six million Jews while the rest of the world stood by idly and did nothing to help. Other nations began to oppose him only when his actions threatened their self-interest.

What a terrible, terrible tragedy! But how very much like Satan. He'll do whatever he can to get his way, whether it involves killing a few hundred babies in ancient Judea or several million Jews in modern Germany.

There are Jews who say they are atheists, who point to the Holocaust and ask how a righteous God could have allowed it to happen. But as far as I'm concerned, this event—although it was a horrible tragedy—demonstrates the reality of God's desire to work through the Jews. If God did not have a special relationship with and definite plans for these people, why would Satan try so hard to get rid of them? And if God were not with them, how could they have survived as a people?

Unfortunately, as I said before, John's vision of the dragon pursuing the woman lets us know that there will be more persecution of the Jews—this time at the hands of the Antichrist. But God will intervene in spectacular ways to vindicate His people, especially those who have accepted Jesus Christ as the Messiah.

The Creature from the Sea

As soon as the vision of the woman and the dragon faded from view, John found himself standing by the sea and watching as a beast rose up out of the water. The sea in the Scriptures is used at times as a symbol of the nations.

> He had ten horns and seven heads, with ten crowns on his horns, and on each head a blasphemous name. The beast I saw resembled a leopard, but had feet like those of a bear and a mouth like that of a lion. The dragon gave the beast his power and his throne and great authority. One of the heads of the beast seemed to have had a fatal wound, but the fatal wound had been healed. The whole world was astonished and followed the beast. Men worshiped the dragon because he had given authority to the beast, and they also worshiped the beast and asked, "Who is like the beast? Who can make war against him?"
>
> Revelation 13:1–4

The description of this Beast with ten horns and seven heads ties in with the description of the great red dragon in the previous chapter. Just as Jesus Christ was God incarnate—as He said, "Anyone who has seen me has seen the Father" (John 14:9)—so the Antichrist will be Satan incarnate. Note how their descriptions match. Compare also the dreadful and awesome beast that Daniel saw in Daniel 7:7–8.

John says that the Beast was given the authority to make war against God's people and to conquer them. He was also "given authority over every tribe, people, language and nation. All inhabitants of the earth will worship the beast—all whose names have not been written in the book of life belonging to the Lamb that was slain from the creation of the world" (verses 7–8).

The Beast that rises out of the sea is the Antichrist, and he will come to power through the efforts of the European Community. It is interesting that the European Community has set 1992 as the year of abolishing their border checks to allow free and unrestricted travel among the nations of Europe. They have also announced that a common European currency will be inaugurated at the same time. Surely we are getting close to the fulfillment of these prophecies from Revelation.

As the symbol for the Soviet Union is the bear, it is possible that "feet of the bear" means that the U.S.S.R. will supply many of the weapons systems he uses in his scheme to bring the world under his control—just as Saddam Hussein's fired relentlessly those highly unreliable Scud missiles he bought from the Soviet Union.

You can be assured, however, that the Soviet Union's status as a world power is going to be severely diminished by the time the Antichrist rises to prominence.

According to the 38th and 39th chapters of Ezekiel, the Russian army is going to invade Israel prior to the Antichrist's arrival on the scene. At first, as Russia moves with all her might against tiny Israel, it will appear that the Jewish homeland is going to be swept away.

But God will move in her behalf. Some five-sixths of the Soviet army will be destroyed. We don't know exactly how it will happen, but God, speaking through Ezekiel, said,

> "I will summon a sword against Gog on all my mountains.
> . . .Every man's sword will be against his brother. I will
> execute judgment upon him with plague and bloodshed;
> I will pour down torrents of rain, hailstones and burning
> sulfur on him and on his troops and on the many nations
> with him. And so I will show my greatness and my holi-
> ness, and I will make myself known in the sight of many
> nations. Then they will know that I am the Lord."
> Ezekiel 38:21–23

Once her army has been destroyed, the Soviet Union will be relegated to the status of a second-class power. She will no longer be a major influence in world affairs. Her destruction will pave the way for the emergence of another power, the European Community, which will consolidate under a single ruler—the Antichrist.

If we turn to the second chapter of Daniel, we find that King Nebuchadnezzar dreamed about the establishment of the Antichrist's kingdom.

In his dream, he saw a great idol with a head of gold, breast and arms of silver, and feet with ten toes made of an iron-and-clay mixture. Daniel explained to the king that this idol represented several kingdoms that would come into power in future years, the toes representing a federation that would come into power last of all.

The ten-nation federation was going to be powerful, but it, too, would be swept into history.

Daniel, interpreting the king's dream, told him: "While you were watching, a rock was cut out, but not by human hands. It struck the statue on its feet of iron and clay and smashed them. Then the iron, the clay, the bronze, the silver and the gold were broken to pieces at the same time and became like chaff on a threshing floor in the summer. The wind swept them away without leaving a trace. But the rock that struck the statue became a huge mountain and filled the whole earth" (Daniel 2:34–35).

In the interpretation of this dream given in Daniel 2:44, it was declared that during the time of the reign of these kings, the God of heaven would set up a Kingdom that shall never be destroyed. Here will be the answer to our prayers that "thy kingdom come. Thy will be done in earth, as it is in heaven" (Matthew 6:10, KJV).

Isaiah, speaking of this day, declared:

> For to us a child is born, to us a son is given, and the government will be on his shoulders. And he will be called Wonderful Counselor, Mighty God, Everlasting Father, Prince of Peace. Of the increase of his government and peace there will be no end. He will reign on David's throne and over his kingdom, establishing and upholding it with justice and righteousness from that time on and forever. The zeal of the Lord Almighty will accomplish this.
>
> Isaiah 9:6–7

Added Daniel, "The dream is true and the interpretation is trustworthy" (Daniel 2:45).

Nebuchadnezzar's dream foretold the rise of the ten-nation federation under the control of the Antichrist, followed by the return of Christ to establish His Kingdom upon the earth. We will talk more about this federation of nations later on.

Regarding the Antichrist's apparently fatal head wound (Revelation 13:3), it is apparent that he will have been critically injured; he may even lose his right eye, and his arm may become paralyzed. In Zechariah 11:17, the prophet says, "Woe to the worthless shepherd, who deserts the flock! May the sword strike his arm and his right eye! May his arm be completely withered, his right eye totally blinded!"

His injury will be so severe that his survival will be regarded as miraculous. This will serve to enhance his status in the eyes of the world.

A Second Beast Appears

Continuing in the thirteenth chapter of Revelation, John receives a vision of another Beast. This one comes out of the earth instead of the sea, and he has "two horns like a lamb, but he spoke like a dragon" (verse 11).

This Beast will force people to worship the first one. He will also perform miraculous signs and wonders, calling down fire from heaven, just as God's two witnesses did before they were martyred. Many people will be convinced that something truly wonderful is happening (again, not knowing that there are two supernatural forces at work in the universe), and will swear their allegiance to the Beast because of these signs and wonders.

After this, the second Beast will order the erection of a great statue "in honor of the beast who was wounded by the sword and yet lived." Once the statue is erected, he gives life and power to it. It begins to speak, commanding for itself worship, and will order the deaths of those who refuse to do so (Revelation 13:14–15).

> He also forced everyone, small and great, rich and poor, free and slave, to receive a mark on his right hand or on his forehead, so that no one could buy or sell unless he had the mark, which is the name of the beast or the number of his name.
> This calls for wisdom. If anyone has insight, let him calculate the number of the beast, for it is man's number. His number is 666.   Revelation 13:16–18

To explain all this, let's go back to the arrival of the Beast who rose out of the sea and, in this instance, represents a multitude of nations. It is out of these nations that the Antichrist will arise.

We will find, as we continue reading in Revelation, that the Beast's seven heads are the seven mountains on which the Beast sits. The ten horns represent ten kings, or ten countries, who will be joined together in allegiance to the Beast, just as Nebuchadnezzar's dream foretold.

Everything Jesus came to do, the Antichrist will seek to undo. Everything Jesus built, he will seek to tear down. Everyone who belongs to Christ, he will seek to destroy.

I talked in the last chapter about God's two witnesses, and how the world will rejoice when these seemingly invincible men are finally killed. The Bible seems to say that the Antichrist will bring about the deaths of these two godly men (Revelation 11:7–10).

This will be another way in which he consolidates his power and wins over the hearts and minds of the people. These two witnesses will wreak much havoc upon this planet, and nobody will be able to stop them. Many men will try, and many men will pay the consequences. But along comes the Antichrist to do the impossible. He will kill them and the world will rejoice.

But this will be possible only because God has allowed it.

It will seem that no one can stand up to the Antichrist: No man, no country, not even the United States with all its might, nor the Soviet Union.

Revelation 13:8 contains an interesting phrase, stating that everyone on the earth will worship the Beast "whose names have not been written in the book of life belonging to the Lamb that was slain from the creation of the world."

Even as He was going about the business of drawing up the blueprints for this planet of ours, God already knew that His Son was going to have to die in our behalf. It's not as if God *wanted* man to fall into sin, or caused it to happen. But He knew that it was going to occur, and He had already devised the only possible way to bring us humans back into proper relationship with Him.

Some people will try to tell you that God doesn't know everything that's going to happen, that He sits back and watches history unfold, and that He gets a few shocks now and then. Well, that's just not true. Nothing happens that surprises God, and He leaves nothing to random chance.

It may appear, in these last days, that God has deserted the earth and that things are totally out of control. Just think about all the "natural" disasters the earth will experience, and how it will be tightly in the grasp of an evil, satanic ruler. But these very events will be bringing God's purposes to pass.

There is a lesson here for any believer who looks at his own life and is tempted to wonder if God has abandoned him to chance, leaving him to spin through life on some gigantic roulette wheel.

No, God does have a plan for your life, and He is in control. What's more, you can know for certain that He has your best interests at heart. He will bring you through whatever bad times come your way, and He'll refine and improve you in the process.

Sometimes it is difficult to see God's hand in circumstances, and to hold onto faith in Him. This is going to be especially true during the last days, when the Antichrist will launch a campaign of bitter persecution against God's people.

As for the second Beast, the one coming out of the earth with two horns like a lamb and with the voice of a dragon, I am reminded once again of Satan's deception. There is one Lamb who was slain for our sins—the Lord Jesus Christ. Yet when this Beast arises from the earth, it too, will have the appearance of a lamb.

What John is saying here is, in effect, "This Beast looked as gentle as a lamb, but it surely didn't act like one." It will be a wolf in sheep's clothing.

Who is this second Beast? He is the Antichrist's faithful lieutenant—his enforcer, so to speak. For just as God will have His two faithful witnesses, Satan will have two henchmen.

We know that this person will be a popular, powerful leader. Perhaps he will be a persuasive orator, like Hitler, able to sway the masses toward belief in the most hideous ideas through the power of his speeches.

Many of us have the wrong idea about Satan, thinking that he must be some hideous, frightening demon. That's far from the truth. Satan is what you might call "a handsome devil." He doesn't have horns, a forked tail, red leotards, and a pitchfork in his hand. He is an attractive creature, appearing as an angel of light (see 2 Corinthians 11:14), and we might say that he is beautiful. In fact, he is described in Ezekiel 28:12 as being "full of wisdom and perfect in beauty."

I once read a news article about an elderly woman who lost several thousand dollars to a con man posing as a bank employee. Lamenting over the loss of her money, she commented, "But he had such an honest face!"

That's Satan: an honest face, but a heart full of lies and deceit.

Sin can fool us, too. We see sin as horrible and ugly, and we define it as murder, robbery, and violence. But often it comes to us as enjoyment and pleasure, whispering, "Go ahead. Stay home Sunday morning and read the paper. You've been working too hard." Or, "Who'll find out if you eat that half-gallon of ice cream this afternoon?" If we aren't careful, sin can suck us in, which is when we discover its horrible, ugly, life-wrecking potential.

John tells us that this second Beast is able, because of the signs and wonders he performs, to deceive the inhabitants of the earth.

In 2 Thessalonians 2:9–12, Paul writes:

> The coming of the lawless one will be in accordance with the work of Satan displayed in all kinds of counterfeit miracles, signs and wonders, and in every sort of evil that deceives those who are perishing. They perish because they refused to love the truth and so be saved. For this reason God sends them a powerful delusion so that they will believe the lie and so that all will be condemned who have not believed the truth but have delighted in wickedness.

Notice the Bible doesn't say that they will believe *a* lie, but rather *the* lie. In other words, they will believe the big lie of Satan: the Antichrist.

People who have rejected the truth of salvation through faith in Jesus Christ will do some amazing things in their search for life's meaning. We see them wearing saffron robes, shaving their heads, and standing on street corners begging passersby for donations. We see them bowing down before the Eastern gurus who take them for every penny they have. And they don't seem to mind.

We see them entering expensive "therapy" where they're locked in a room for a weekend, abused verbally, and not even allowed to leave for bathroom breaks. And we see them falling for the Satan-inspired chicanery of those who pretend to be "channels" for the spirits of ancient wise men.

It's all terrible stupidity, yet millions of souls are sinking slowly in the quicksand of religious quackery.

Those who reject the truth will almost always wind up investing their minds and energies in support of a lie.

Life with the Seekers

Several years ago I was invited to meet with the "intelligentsia" of Orange County, California—several college professors and doctors who got together every so often to discuss the meaning of life and to share their new insights and philosophies.

I suppose they had talked about everything else, so they decided to invite a Christian pastor into their midst. They had heard of Calvary Chapel and knew we were attracting large crowds to our services. Some members of this group may have thought I had a small kernel of truth to share, but I'm sure that others were interested only in poking fun at an ignoramus who actually believed in a living God who created the heavens and the earth. I was skeptical about the invitation, but I didn't want to turn down a chance to witness for the Lord.

Before the meeting began, one of the group's leaders, sitting on the floor in the lotus position, began to tell me all about his many accomplishments—the philosophers he had studied, the gurus he had sat under, the scholarly papers he had written. He

said he was a Buddhist priest, but that this did not mean he
would automatically reject any truths that Christianity might
have to offer. In fact, he spent so much time telling me how
open-minded he was that I began to suspect his mind was
locked up tighter than a vault at Fort Knox.

He told me he and the other members of the group considered themselves to be "seekers," interested only in finding the
truth. This search for "enlightenment" seemed to have taken
them everywhere, even into serious experimentation with LSD.
But it had not, so far, included an exploration of the life and
claims of Jesus Christ.

It's funny, but it seems to be human nature to reject the truth
that stares us right in the face.

"You've done a lot of searching," I told the group. "But the
fact that you call yourselves seekers tells me you haven't found
what you're looking for. Maybe you've overlooked something."

Then I started with the basics. I told them that in the beginning God had created the heavens and the earth.

Before I could get any further, someone interrupted me:
"Now when you say 'God,' are you talking about an an-
thropomorphic concept of God?"

Immediately another member of the group challenged his
statement, precipitating a long argument, mostly involving
words that William F. Buckley would have had to look up in
the dictionary.

While this war of words raged around me I bowed my head
and began to pray: *Lord God, if You just get me through this
and out of this place, I promise I'll never come back here again.
I realize that I've been neglecting my wife. I haven't been spending enough time at home. My kids don't get a chance to see their
father, and here I am, spending an evening in a place like this.
Help me, Lord. I don't know what to say to get through to these
people.*

Just as I finished my prayer, one of the women in the group
got fed up with her arguing fellow-seekers.

"Will you guys shut up! We hear you all the time, and every week it's the same inane arguments. We invited this fellow to speak to us, so the least we can do is listen to him."

Thank you, lady, and thank You, Lord.

The men stopped arguing, apologized, and told me I had the floor.

Then I knew what to say.

I looked around the room. "My soul and my spirit are at rest," I said. "I am completely satisfied."

It was amazing how quickly they all began to sit up and pay attention. None of them could say that. Despite all their intelligence, wisdom, and searching, there was not a satisfied soul in the room.

For the next hour I shared with them the richness and fullness that can be experienced through Jesus Christ. I didn't try to relate to them on an intellectual basis, because they would have argued and picked at what I was saying all night long. But there was no way they could argue with the peace and joy that Jesus Christ brings.

No shattering changes took place that night, but in the succeeding weeks several of those men and women came by to see me, and wound up surrendering their lives to Christ. They were now ready to exchange a lie for the truth.

These were intelligent, capable people, and it amazed me that they had been misled for so long. But because they had refused to believe the truth, God had given them over to lies and deception. And this is exactly what will happen when the Antichrist arrives on the world scene.

The Statue that Comes to Life

What about the statue of the first Beast that comes to life? Up until the last few years, this passage has been difficult to understand. Who ever heard of a statue coming to life?

But now the technology required to make this possible is just around the corner. It's called genetic engineering, or artificial intelligence.

Some scientists believe it's the next step in the computer revolution, and that's another good reason for believing that this vision of John will take place in the near future.

Computers are amazing. They can calculate intricate math problems in a fraction of a second; store reams of information available for recall at the touch of a button; and perform any number of other functions that make the human mind seem puny by comparison.

Computers are so smart, we're almost tempted to think they're alive. They aren't. At least, not yet. But someday they may be.

Even now, scientists are talking about gene-splicing, genetic codes, and DNA patterns that they hope to use to develop computers into living creatures. I don't pretend to come close to understanding the processes involved, but the basic idea would be to "sew together" the computer memory with the genetic code necessary for the existence of life.

Imagine these computer-people working in our homes. They'd never need to be fed, and they'd never complain or ask for a raise. They'd need only occasional maintenance, and they'd even be able to reproduce themselves so we wouldn't have to worry about buying new ones when the old ones wore out.

Scientists tell us that when this bright day comes, there will be no danger of a computer revolt, the subject of science fiction speculation for many years. Even though these computers could learn to "think" for themselves should the need arise, they'll still be under our control, the scientists tell us, and still dependent upon their human masters.

One wonders how they can be so sure, considering all the horrors that have come from scientific "advancement" throughout the years. The development of nuclear power, for example, promised many life-enhancing spin-offs, but Satan used that advance to give us weapons of unbelievably destructive power. Look at the development of lasers, which has prompted amazing new surgical and communications techniques. But now lasers, too, are being used in weapons development, and we hear talk of satellites firing "death beams" from outer space.

Yes, there has been an ugly, evil side to every scientific breakthrough or advancement, making me wonder how scientists can be so sure this won't happen with the concept of genetic engineering—especially in light of what John is saying here in the thirteenth chapter of Revelation.

I believe the statue of the Antichrist will be a computerized replica of the evil world ruler. Just imagine a being with all the intelligence and capacity of the world's most advanced computer combined with all the evil, cunning, and power of Satan himself.

This computer-creature will be placed in the Holy of Holies of the rebuilt Temple, and people will be commanded to bow down and worship it. There will be a simple choice to make: Worship or die.

This is the "abomination that causes desolation" (Daniel 12:11). In other words, it is the last straw, after which God will begin to pour out His fury and judgment upon the earth.

As for the Antichrist, he now begins his plan to place his number on the right hands or foreheads of all who will pledge allegiance to him. John says that no one anywhere will be allowed to buy or sell unless he has this mark, the number of the Beast—666.

When John talks of the Beast's number being placed on people's bodies, my mind turns once again to Adolf Hitler. He had Jews rounded up as if they were so many cattle and tattooed—branded. I've seen these tattoos on the bodies of some who managed to survive Hitler's death camps, and I've shuddered for two reasons:

First, because this is a reminder of how cruel human beings can be to one another when they listen to the lies of Satan.

Second, because this is a foretaste of things to come. The same Satan who influenced Hitler will also control the Antichrist. The terror of Hitler's regime was simply a trial run for the reign of the Antichrist, and that's a horrible thought. There is no limit to Satan's evil.

The numbers that will be placed on the bodies of those living during the time of the Tribulation will reflect technological advancement over the tattoos placed on the bodies of Hitler's prisoners. Once again Satan will take advantage of new technology to further the establishments of his kingdom.

And no one will be able to buy or sell unless he has the mark of the Beast. One day I was in a grocery store checkout line when a woman ahead of me wanted to write a check for her purchases. She had the check all made out when the clerk asked to see her driver's license.

"I don't have one," the woman said.

"You don't have a driver's license?" the clerk asked in a shocked tone of voice.

"I don't drive."

"Well, I'm sorry, but I don't think I can take this check without a driver's license."

Much to the anger of those waiting in line behind me, this prompted a lengthy discussion involving the customer, the cashier, the store's assistant manager, and then the manager himself. The woman's check was finally accepted, but she was advised to go to the Department of Motor Vehicles and get what must amount to a driver's license for non-drivers!

As I listened to the discussion, I realized that it's almost impossible to buy and sell today unless we have some sort of identification number, whether it's a driver's license, a Social Security number, or national credit card. And since most people are already accustomed to this, the Antichrist won't face as much resistance regarding his new "numbering plan" as we might think.

But I believe more than identification is at stake in this plan. I believe these numbers will act like credit cards. People will go into a store or bank and some sort of scanner will read their numbers. The store's computers will be able to identify each customer, and tell how much credit he or she has available. There will be no need for cash in this society, and this will be hailed as a tremendous breakthrough of safety and convenience. But the system's main purpose will be to control and monitor the population at all times.

The technology for this cashless society is already in place. For several years now supermarkets all across the country have been phasing out their old cash registers in favor of scanners that read computer price codes. The cashier runs the item across the scanner, it beeps, and the price is displayed on the cash register screen.

You know as well as I do that they haven't perfected the process. You try to buy a loaf of bread, and the cashier runs it across the scanner. No beep. She runs it across again. Still no beep. Finally on the third or fourth try you hear the familiar beep and see the price—or else the exasperated checker enters the price manually. Meanwhile, you're lucky if your bread isn't squashed into a lopsided mess! There are still a few kinks to be worked out before a cashless society is the sort of system an evil world ruler could be proud of.

I've also been reading about the new "smartcards" and the ease they can bring to your life. They look just like Visa or MasterCard, but when you buy something with them their microchips immediately tally up your balance. If you're over your credit limit—sorry, no sale. Other credit cards deduct the amount charged directly from your bank account. You don't have to carry cash around, you don't have to write a check, and you won't get any bills at the end of the month. Many banks, buried under an avalanche of paper, are trying to get their customers to use these cards instead of writing checks. There has also been talk about implanting computer chips under the skin in a person's hand so he can be quickly and easily identified. Another new technology has been announced featuring a scanner that can read the vein pattern on the back of your hand, which is as unique as your thumbprint. The code for this pattern can be placed on your credit card, providing a foolproof system to keep someone else from using your card.

All these developments cause us to realize that the day a person cannot buy or sell without an I.D. on the back of his hand is not far away. And if you hear suggestions like these without getting a chill down your spine, you obviously haven't been reading the book of Revelation.

Now please don't think I'm suggesting that all these new technologies are evil or that they're inspired by Satan. I don't want anyone going into his neighborhood supermarket and trying to cast demons out of the cash register. My point is not that these things are evil in and of themselves; rather, that they are the framework of the technology the Antichrist will use to further his purposes. Systems designed to make our lives easier, or to give us more freedom, he will use to control and enslave.

I've talked to people who were nearly ready to burn their Social Security cards because they were concerned that they might have given in to the mark of the Beast. Other people won't use automatic tellers at their banks for the same reason.

But the sin does not lie in the technology itself. Those who accept the mark of the Beast will know exactly what they're doing. This numbering system will be instituted by a world ruler opposed to God and everything He stands for. Those who accept the mark will know that to do this is to accept the leadership of the Antichrist and, in essence, pledge allegiance to him.

Not all of them will know they are pledging allegiance to Satan as well. Many will undoubtedly view the Antichrist as a wonderful man who has brought peace to the planet and who deserves their adoration. But even here they will know that acceptance of his mark is also acceptance of his authority over them.

The mark of the Beast is much more than a mark or number. It is a symbol of the leader who possesses your heart, mind, and soul.

Looking for 666

In the final verse of the thirteenth chapter, we find these words:

> This calls for wisdom. If anyone has insight, let him calculate the number of the beast, for it is man's number. His number is 666.

This particular verse has been the subject of a great deal of speculation over the years, some of it bordering on lunacy. The finger has been pointed at any and every leader whose name can be made to add up to 666 in one way or another. Among those who have been singled out as the Antichrist are Adolf Hitler and Benito Mussolini—both of whom were understandable candidates in their day—John F. Kennedy, Henry Kissinger, and Ronald Reagan.

I remember that when John Kennedy was elected President, many Protestant churchmen spoke out against him. I'm sad to say that much of the opposition was based on the fact that he was a Roman Catholic. It seems strange, looking back on it from the vantage point of nearly thirty years later, but there was fear that John Kennedy was going to sell out the American people to the Vatican.

Even after President Kennedy was assassinated, there were some who insisted that this proved that their choice of him as the Antichrist was correct. They pointed to the Scriptures talking about the Beast recovering from the fatal head wound, and they waited for John Kennedy to return to life.

But he was not the Antichrist. Nor was Henry Kissinger, who was nominated for the position simply because some did not care for his politics.

To peg Kennedy or Kissinger as the Antichrist, you had to play fast and loose with the numbers. By assigning each letter in the name a numerical value and then dividing by the number of letters, throwing in a few square roots and algebraic equations, each of these names can be made to calculate out to 666. Actually, I believe you could make anyone's name total 666 if you worked at it long enough.

It's a bit easier for those who want to brand Ronald Reagan as the son of perdition. After all, there are six letters in each of his three names: Ronald Wilson Reagan. But Ronald Reagan is not the Antichrist.

So the question persists: What does 666 mean?

You may know that in the Bible every number has significance. For instance, twelve is the number of human government, thirteen the number of Satan, and seven the number of completeness or perfection. Six is the number of man, who is less than perfect. Man came into being on the sixth day of creation. The number six signifies, then, that the Antichrist is going to be a human being.

This is more meaningful in Hebrew and Greek than it is in English, because both of those languages also count with their letters. In other words, in Greek *alpha, beta, gamma, delta* mean A, B, C, and D, but they also mean one, two, three, and four. Because every Greek letter has a numeric equivalent, we can easily total up the numerical value of a word.

For instance, eight is the number of new beginnings, and if we compute the numerical value of the name *Jesus* it will add up to eight, eight, eight. If we take all the names of Jesus and total up all the letters, we'll always come up with a total divisible by eight. Conversely, if we take *Satan,* or any of the names for Satan, we will come up with a number divisible by 13.

So it is true that the Antichrist's name will add up to 666, or to a numerical value divisible by six. In chapters still to come, John gives a few more clues as to the identity of this man, but as yet we have no idea who he will be. My own feeling is that he is probably alive and well on planet earth right now, but that he hasn't come to prominence. He may be in his twenties or thirties, or he may be in his teens. He may be a mere child, taking his first shaky steps in the world he is one day going to conquer.

I wish I knew where and who he is. But even if we knew his name, I feel certain it wouldn't mean anything to us. He may be biding his time, consolidating his strength, waiting for the time to be right. He may even now be the mastermind behind certain terrorist strikes but he is still a ways from bursting onto the world scene.

Meanwhile, those of us who are walking with God need not have an inordinate fear of the number 666. We don't have to hyperventilate every time we see it, or panic if the phone company assigns us that telephone exchange. If we stay close to God, pray for wisdom, and keep our eyes open, we will almost certainly learn the identity of the Antichrist as he begins his ascendancy to power.

7

Help Is on the Way

Revelation 14–15

Do you remember the days when every movie theater in town had a special Saturday matinee? It was usually a double feature, preceded by at least half-a-dozen cartoons and a chapter or two of a continuing serial—and it was the dream of many a harried mother. She could drop her kids off a little after noon, and not have to return to pick them up until 5:30 or six o'clock. So long as the kids had a few quarters for Bon-Bons, popcorn, and a soda or two, they would have a fine afternoon—and so, most likely, would Mom.

She might not feel too good about the junk food they were going to eat, but she knew the movies would be wholesome stories with a moral. Oh, there might be a little violence (although it was nothing like we see in movies today), but the good guys always won and the bad guys usually learned a valuable lesson.

It was just about always true in those days that the bad guys appeared for most of the picture to be winning. Squirming in their seats, the kids all wondered how long this could go on. Were the bad guys going to win one for a change?

Sooner or later, there came a point when things looked their absolute darkest. The good guy might be tied to a chair in an old shack, and the camera panned down to show three or four sticks of dynamite on the floor beneath him. And that's not all—the fuse was lit, and burning furiously.

Was this going to be it for Mr. Good Guy?

No way! Just as all the kids in the front row were covering their eyes, they'd hear the telltale music that signaled help was on the way. Just in time, an entire posse would rush into the room to throw the dynamite out the window before it exploded. They'd quickly untie their good guy colleague, learn from him what the bad guys were up to, and round up all the crooks in a matter of minutes.

Well, I hope nobody misunderstands me. Life is no movie. But Satan is definitely like those old movie villains. Everywhere he turns, he's thwarted again, but he simply will not give up.

"This time I'm going to win," he says, rubbing his hands together in glee. But every time he winds up disappointed. That's the way it's always been for him, and that's the way it's always going to be.

God is very much like that old motion picture cavalry that always arrived just in the nick of time.

It's that way in the personal lives of God's people, and will be like that with the entire world when the end of the age arrives.

Recounting the victories God has helped you to win gives you more faith to believe Him for victory in the battles ahead. And when others hear what God has done in your life, they become excited because they know He can do the same thing for them.

In all the testimonies I've heard over the years, I can't possibly count how many times I've heard someone say, "I had really reached the bottom," or, "I was at the end of my rope," or, "I couldn't have lasted for another minute."

It always seems God is stepping in at the last possible moment, just when we're about to give up or when there is no alternative but to lean on Him.

And it is true now, in Revelation 13, with all mankind tottering on the brink, about to plunge into eternal darkness, along with the planet he has called home for thousands of years. But it's never too late for the Lamb of God, Jesus Christ, to step in and save the day.

As we enter the fourteenth chapter of Revelation, John takes a look at God's holy mountain, Mount Zion. And what he sees must take his breath away, for there is the Lamb of God, the Conqueror, surrounded by 144,000 of His people—those who have His name and the Father's name written on their foreheads. Satan thinks he is having a field day, but the cavalry is on its way!

> Then I looked, and there before me was the Lamb, standing on Mount Zion, and with him 144,000 who had his name and his Father's name written on their foreheads. And I heard a sound from heaven like the roar of rushing waters and like a loud peal of thunder. The sound I heard was like that of harpists playing their harps. And they sang a new song before the throne and before the four living creatures and the elders. No one could learn the song except the 144,000 who had been redeemed from the earth. These are those who did not defile themselves with women, for they kept themselves pure. They follow the Lamb wherever he goes. They were purchased from among men and offered as firstfruits to God and the Lamb. No lie was found in their mouths; they are blameless.
>
> Revelation 14:1–5

And now John sees another angel flying in the midst of heaven, and he has the everlasting Gospel to preach to those who live on the earth, "every nation, tribe, language and people" (verse 6).

There are those who believe that what John saw flying in heaven was not an angelic being at all, but a satellite. They say that there was no way for a man from the first century to understand a satellite except to say that it was an angel.

Now I applaud any effort to spread the Gospel, and I am

especially grateful for those who are using the latest technology, including communications satellites, to reach the lost. But, having said that, I'll still have to say that I don't think this is what John is talking about. My own belief is that this is an actual angel, one of God's messengers who has come to fulfill the Word of God and to see that the Gospel is preached throughout all the world.

Remember the words of Jesus: "And this gospel of the kingdom will be preached in the whole world as a testimony to all nations, and then the end will come" (Matthew 24:14).

Some Christians believe that we can speed up the return of Jesus by strengthening our efforts to preach the Gospel throughout the world. After all, Jesus said that as soon as all nations have heard the Gospel, the end will come.

I believe, however, that this is a misinterpretation of Christ's words. While I admire anyone who wants to preach the Gospel, and am delighted to hear of ministries that are taking the Word of God into the remotest parts of Africa, Asia, and South America, I still have to believe that these efforts will not be totally successful until the time of the Tribulation.

Does this mean we should abandon our efforts to reach the world with the Gospel? Of course not, because those efforts are worth it if they keep just one soul from spending eternity in hell. At the same time, I do not believe we can speed up Christ's return by speeding up our missionary efforts, nor can we keep Him from coming back by scaling down our mission programs. The timing for these events has already been arranged by God almighty.

How will this message be preached to all the world? I'm not sure. There may be groups of resistance fighters who realize that the best way to fight the Antichrist will be to preach the Gospel. If so, they will be able to use some of the facilities and technologies—albeit outdated ones—left behind by Christians who have been raptured. They may transmit poor-quality sound and pictures—but they will transmit to a world hungry to know the truth and growing weary of the Antichrist's lies.

Here in America, where there are churches on practically every street corner, dozens of Christian TV and radio stations, and bookstores full of Bibles, people take religion for granted. They yawn, stretch, and respond, "Oh, yes, it's nice that Christ died for my sins, thank you, but I've planned an afternoon at the beach, so don't bother me now."

In the Soviet Union, on the other hand, Christians protect and cherish little torn pieces of the Bible as if they were precious diamonds. And that's what they are, because the average Russian citizen has little way to obtain a complete Bible. He holds onto what he can get and is overjoyed to get it.

Russian believers risk prison in many instances, even in these days of *glasnost,* just for believing in God and for wanting their children to do the same. They endure harassment, loss of prestige, and loss of employment, and they do it gladly in service to the King.

I believe that this is the way it will be when the Gospel is preached to the entire world during the days of Tribulation.

Today, when the Gospel is being shouted loudly from the housetops, we find many people who hear what we're saying but don't listen. During the Tribulation, all this will change.

An evangelistic zeal will burn as never before on this planet, with the possible exception of what happened in Jerusalem on the Day of Pentecost shortly after the resurrection and ascension of Christ. I envision families in the remotest parts of the earth—perhaps even entire communities—huddled around old radios for a chance to hear the Gospel, knowing that they're risking their lives, but also that the risk is worth it.

Within the last few years the world's population has climbed past the five billion mark. It is said that more than half of the people have never had a chance to hear about the saving grace of Jesus Christ. What's more, the percentage of the population that has never heard of Christ seems to be increasing, with most of the world's population growth taking place in third-world countries—places like China, India, and Africa. There, despite modern technology and the best efforts of dedicated believers, the Gospel has not yet penetrated to any degree.

I do believe that our efforts today are bearing fruit and paving the way for the worldwide revival that will occur in the last days. In the meantime, we can only keep on working, knowing that one day soon the last barriers will fall and the Word will spread rapidly throughout all the earth.

As John continues to watch the angel carrying the Gospel, the angel says in a loud voice,

> "Fear God and give him glory, because the hour of his judgment has come. Worship him who made the heavens, the earth, the sea and the springs of water."
>
> Revelation 14:7

The angel commands people to worship God who made the universe, rather than the universe itself. Today so many people worship the creation rather than the Creator. Scientists talk about the "universal Mind," the way "nature" adapts to change, and so on, while they refuse to acknowledge God. Some scientists have come to view the universe as a gigantic computer that stores and analyzes information, yet they disdain any talk of God. They'll tell you that this gigantic universal Mind guided the development of life and has somehow been involved with the "evolution" of man throughout the millennia, but they still don't believe in God.

It interests me that in the days of the Industrial Revolution, scientists looked at the universe and saw an exact replica of their society's cannibalistic world of business and unrestrained capitalism, in which only the strongest survived. Charles Darwin took this principle, applied it to nature, and called it "survival of the fittest." It became one of the main tenets of his theory of evolution.

Darwin observed that businesses that did not adapt to changing times died out, and that only those able to adapt and conform to the latest technology enjoyed long-term success. He claimed similarly ruthless competition in the animal world, with new and better species evolving and the old and non-adaptable dying out—a pretty big leap, but Darwin made it.

That was the nineteenth century.

The Industrial Revolution is over, but the twentieth century's informational revolution is on, and its centerpiece is the computer. So modern man looks at the universe and—surprise!—sees a gigantic computer. The universe is loaded with information and intelligence, but it is mindless, he says, in much the same way that a computer is mindless.

It's strange that men who are confronted with the complexity, intelligence, and order of the universe still insist on worshiping the creation instead of the Creator. In that sense, man as a species hasn't come very far from the days when he made sacrifices to appease volcanoes and rivers.

The complexity of creation testifies to the fact that there is a Creator, and the angel in Revelation 14 calls the whole world to worship Him.

Another angel follows immediately with a different message. This time the news is that "Babylon" has fallen—Babylon, the great city that made all the nations drink of the "maddening wine of her adulteries" (Revelation 14:8).

Who or what is Babylon? We'll know more about that when we come to chapter 17. For now I'll just say that she is a religious and commercial empire of vast proportions.

And now John tells us of a third angel, who says in a loud voice:

> "If anyone worships the beast and his image and receives
> his mark on the forehead or on the hand, he, too, will
> drink of the wine of God's fury, which has been poured
> full strength into the cup of his wrath."
>
> Revelation 14:9–10

As I said before, no one will take the mark of the Beast without knowing what it represents. People will be warned of the consequences, but that won't deter many of them. They will be fooled to the extent that they choose to believe the Antichrist rather than God, just as many people today choose the temporary pleasures of Satan over the lasting pleasures of Jesus Christ.

But no believer will be able to think, *I'll let them put the mark on me, but God will know I don't really worship the Beast and He'll forgive me. It's just to help me buy food for my family.* God has made it very clear that His wrath will be poured out upon all who take the mark upon themselves.

It's not going to be easy to refuse the mark. In the first place, those who do so are going to suffer persecution at the hands of the Antichrist, even to the point of being put to death. Second, unless a person receives the mark, he won't be able to buy a thing.

Some believing fathers and mothers will be torn as they realize that, without the mark, it will be almost impossible for them to feed their children—unless God provides miraculously. This will be a time of great testing and persecution, when only those who are truly committed to God will be able to withstand the terrors of the Antichrist's system.

We live in a society that thrives on buying on credit, and it makes me wonder if millions of people won't accept the mark of the Beast realizing they'll have to pay later for doing so. Their attitude will be, "I know I'm going to have to suffer one way or another, but at least I'm buying a little time." Very little time. And the suffering to come later is hardly worth a little expedience now.

It sounds horrible, but the angel says that anyone who receives the mark of the Beast

> "will be tormented with burning sulfur in the presence of the holy angels and of the Lamb. And the smoke of their torment rises for ever and ever. There is no rest day or

night for those who worship the beast and his image, or
for anyone who receives the mark of his name."

Revelation 14:10–11

Then he quickly adds, in verse 12,

"This calls for patient endurance on the part of the saints
who obey God's commandments and remain faithful to
Jesus."

Does God's punishment seem unjust? Just remember that He
is going to give everyone on earth the opportunity to turn away
from the Antichrist and worship Him alone. He is going to
proclaim the Gospel to everyone. He will warn people what will
happen to them if they accept the mark of the Beast.

Yet there will still be active, open rebellion against God.
There will be a final rejection of Him on the part of many people
who will be saying, in essence, that they know what God expects of them, but they're not going to do it. They'll be like
bratty little children, thumbing their noses at God and daring
Him to do anything about it. And He is simply not going to put
up with it.

What about those who are faithful to the end?

Then I heard a voice from heaven say, "Write: Blessed are
the dead who die in the Lord from now on."

"Yes," says the Spirit, "they will rest from their labor,
for their deeds will follow them."   Revelation 14:13

And now John sees another vision of Jesus Christ. This time
He is seated on a white cloud. He is wearing a crown of gold
on His head and has a sharp sickle in His hand. He is going to
take His sickle and reap the earth, because "the harvest of the
earth is ripe" (verses 14–15).

Jesus thrusts His sickle over the earth and begins to reap. He gathers grapes that are thrown into the winepress of God's wrath, and as they are trampled, John tells us that "blood flowed out of the press, rising as high as the horses' bridles for a distance of 1,600 stadia" (verse 20)—or approximately 180 miles.

You see, Jesus Christ is about to return to this earth. The Antichrist knows this. His top generals know it. By now all the people in the world will have made informed decisions as to whose side they are on—God's or Satan's. And the armies of the world, which are under the control of the Antichrist, will come together in an effort to stop Jesus Christ from coming back.

How foolish! They actually think they can use armed might to deter the hand of God, and to keep the Son of God from returning to this planet which He purchased through the shedding of His own blood.

When this happens, Jesus will defeat them as easily as if He were plucking fat, juicy grapes off a vine and tossing them into a winepress. The prophet Isaiah recorded this same scene as God, speaking through him, says:

> "I have trodden the winepress alone; from the nations no one was with me. I trampled them in my anger and trod them down in my wrath; their blood spattered my garments, and I stained all my clothing. For the day of vengeance was in my heart, and the year of my redemption has come. I looked, but there was no one to help, I was appalled that no one gave support; so my own arm worked salvation for me, and my own wrath sustained me. I trampled the nations in my anger; in my wrath I made them drunk and poured their blood on the ground."
>
> Isaiah 63:3–6

Isaiah also explains God's wrath:

> In his love and mercy he redeemed them; he lifted them
> up and carried them all the days of old. Yet they rebelled
> and grieved his Holy Spirit. So he turned and became their
> enemy and he himself fought against them.
>
> Isaiah 63:9–10

Because God's wrath is completed, John now sees seven angels ready with the seven last plagues to be poured out upon the earth. As these angels prepare to carry out their duties, John sees, standing beside the sea, those who have been victorious over the Beast and his image.

These people are probably the same ones John mentions in Revelation 6, when the fifth seal was opened and he saw those souls under the altar crying, "How long, Sovereign Lord, holy and true, until you judge the inhabitants of the earth and avenge our blood?" They were told to rest for a little while until their number was complete.

That has apparently been accomplished now, and we see them standing by the sea of glass as they wait to see God avenge their blood that was shed by martyrdom.

As they sing, they are declaring the justice of God, proclaiming that He is doing exactly what is right as He prepares to bring final judgment upon the planet.

As John continues to watch the scene unfold, seven angels come out of the Temple, all dressed in "clean, shining linen" and wearing golden sashes around their chests. Each of these angels is given a golden bowl filled with the wrath of God.

If the Antichrist and his followers want to fight against God, they are making a mistake of major proportions.

The good guys are about to triumph. The bad guys will be blown away.

8

Assault on the Antichrist

Revelation 16

The Antichrist seems to be invincible. He has conquered the entire world with ease—something no other military genius has ever been able to do, not Alexander the Great, not Napoleon, not Hitler. He is the most powerful leader the world has ever seen, and there seems to be no way to stop him. He crushes anyone who stands in his way, and he will tolerate no disobedience.

The Antichrist and his generals believe they have established a kingdom that will stand forever and ever. Hitler looked for the thousand-year reign of his Third Reich. His dreams were puny in comparison with those of this latter-day conqueror.

But the Antichrist hasn't figured the wrath of God into his equation. Those who dare to shake their fists in God's face are playing a dangerous game. No one can stand up to the might and power of God, not even the Antichrist, who has all the forces and power of Satan at his disposal. His mighty kingdom is about to wash away like so much wet sand in the face of God's anger.

In the last chapter, we noted seven angels coming out of the Temple, each of them being given a golden bowl containing the wrath of God. Now the command is given for these bowls, the final judgments of God, to be poured out.

> Then I heard a loud voice from the temple saying to the seven angels, "Go, pour out the seven bowls of God's wrath on the earth."

The first angel went and poured out his bowl on the
land, and ugly and painful sores broke out on the people
who had the mark of the beast and worshiped his image.
Revelation 16:1–2

God will make a distinction between His people and the
people who have pledged their allegiance to the Antichrist.
God's people will suffer during this period of the earth's history,
but their suffering will never come from the hand of God. They
may receive persecution and martyrdom at the hands of the evil
world government because of their faith in God. But they are
spared the wrath of God, which is far more terrible than anything the Antichrist could do to them.

These sores that form upon the Antichrist's followers will
apparently be great, running ulcers, the sort of thing you would
get from radiation burns.

It could be that something will go wrong with the Beast's
numbering system, causing people to become ill. Maybe the
boils will result from radiation poisoning, caused by the scan-
ning devices used to read the numbers whenever someone wants
to buy or sell something. Perhaps some accident will occur in
his storehouse of chemical and biological weapons, thus unleashing these terrible diseases on his "loyal" subjects.

They may also be related to the depletion of the earth's
protective ozone layer. Scientists have been warning us for
years that the ozone layer, which serves as a natural filter for
the dangerous ultraviolet rays that are a part of ordinary sunlight, is getting thinner, and that it is, in essence, getting holes
in it.

If you've ever spent too much time lying in the sun, you know
what ultraviolet rays can do—because those rays produce both
tanning and burning. Your sunburn would have been more
painful, however, if there were no ozone layer to block out the
majority of the sun's ultraviolet rays.

But the ozone layer sits there, forty miles up, like a protective blanket God has thrown around the planet. Another wonderful "coincidence" as far as the atheist is concerned, it is to me another obvious sign of God's grace and love. He has thought of and given us everything we need on this planet.

But now, we are told, we've been damaging the ozone layer by means of pollution, allowing more ultraviolet light waves through. The layer over the South Pole has already been well eaten into; recently it was discovered that the layer over the North Pole is starting to be eaten away as well. Apparently one of the principal causes is the use of fluorocarbons, which are found in some air fresheners, hairsprays, deodorants, and spray paints. Whenever we use sprays that contain them, they are released to collect just underneath the ozone layer like so many tiny moths under a wool blanket. This is not good news for the human race.

Since the controversy over fluorocarbons began, some manufacturers have stopped using them. The backs of many spray cans now carry the words *Contains no fluorocarbons.* Most manufacturers are not admitting that fluorocarbons are harmful, but they want you to know they've gone the extra mile to remove them from their products.

The question is, have these actions come too late?

Some scientists say yes, others no. Still others believe that the danger was blown out of proportion, that fluorocarbons aren't the villains they've been made out to be.

It's not my intention to take sides in the fluorocarbon debate, but I do know that ultraviolet rays can do all sorts of damage. In addition to burning the skin, they can cause skin cancer, including the potentially deadly melanoma, and they are especially hard on the eyes.

I also know that God put the ozone layer in our atmosphere to protect us, and if we are going to poke holes in it, we are definitely going to reap the consequences.

These speculations would be "natural" ways of explaining why only those with the mark of the Beast become sick. Of course, God doesn't need any help, and it could be that He has simply protected His people supernaturally from whatever is causing the boils, just as He did in Egypt thousands of years ago.

The Contamination of Water

> The second angel poured out his bowl on the sea, and it turned into blood like that of a dead man, and every living thing in the sea died.
> The third angel poured out his bowl on the rivers and springs of water, and they became blood. Then I heard the angel in charge of the waters say:
> "You are just in these judgments, you who are and who were, the Holy One, because you have so judged; for they have shed the blood of your saints and prophets, and you have given them blood to drink as they deserve."
>
> Revelation 16:3–6

The second and third angels will cause disaster to befall the earth's water. How they will do this is, once again, a matter of speculation. Could it be that man himself will be a part of the problem?

Think of all the news reports over the last few years about problems with the disposal of toxic waste. Some companies have been dumping the vilest poisons into the water.

And while we've cleaned up some of our lakes and rivers over the last few years, and have more government regulations and agencies aimed at controlling pollution, the chemicals we're polluting with today are much more dangerous than those used even fifteen years ago.

It's an example of a little bit going a long, long way. Maybe one or two horrendous accidents will pollute large sections of ocean. Perhaps a huge chain reaction will begin—a plague scientists can find no way to stop, and which will in a matter of months destroy all ocean life.

Or perhaps it will have nothing at all to do with man's negligence.

In his book *Worlds in Collision* (Pocket Books, 1977), researcher Immanuel Velikovsky puts forth some interesting theories about the planet Venus.

He speculates that Venus first became part of our solar system just a few thousand years ago. Before that it was a huge piece of debris hurtling through space all by itself. But as it was pulled into orbit around the sun, it came dangerously close to the earth.

So close, in fact, that the earth itself was pulled out of its orbit. To back this up, Velikovsky points to the fact that ancient man figured the year as a 360-day cycle, whereas we know today that it actually takes 365¼ days for the earth to go around the sun. Most scientists assume that this is the way it has always been, that ancient man was simply incorrect in his calculations. Velikovsky disagrees. He believes that the old calendar was right until Venus came along and changed things.

He also believes that as Venus passed close to us, parts of the planet were broken off and pulled into the earth's atmosphere. As this space debris disintegrated, he theorizes, it caused a blanket of red dust to cover much of the earth. He goes so far as to suggest that this "close encounter" with Venus occurred during the time when the plagues were falling on the land of Egypt. The red dust turned the oceans and lakes into "blood" and made fresh water undrinkable.

I'm not suggesting that Velikovsky's theories are correct, but they are at least plausible. As I've said before, we know that there are several thousand asteroids in our solar system. Approximately two thousand of them have orbits that could occasionally bring them within several thousand miles of the earth.

Even if the theory about Venus is incorrect, this scenario could conceivably happen in the future. An asteroid (or even several asteroids) could come within the earth's gravitational pull. Perhaps it would disintegrate as it entered our atmosphere, or perhaps it would plow into the earth, raising a dust cloud that could be seen for hundreds of miles. Either way, it would fill our air with dust and space debris that would settle upon the oceans. This, in turn, could produce a worldwide red tide and destroy all sea life.

Those of us who live along the beaches of California—or along the coast anywhere, I suppose—know about a red tide and the havoc it can play with sea life. Every once in a while we see news stories about fishermen, crabbers, or oystermen complaining that a red tide is destroying their livelihood. We also see stories warning us not to eat certain seafoods that were harvested during a red tide.

A natural red tide is caused by the overmultiplication of plankton and other microscopic sea creatures. These creatures turn the water a reddish color and release toxins that kill other forms of sea life. When a red tide is in progress, as many as 50 million of these little creatures may live in a single quart of water.

As far as I'm concerned, a red tide makes for a beautiful picture. I love to go down to the beach at night and watch the surf because it looks like it's full of little neon tubes. Southern California plankton contain a great deal of phosphorus, and as the waves roll them over, they light up. It's really a magical sight . . . as long as you don't think about all the damage it's doing.

The water itself tastes horrible if you should swallow some. And if you get it in your eyes, it feels as if someone poured soap in them. As the red tide progresses, dead fish come in with the surf.

Usually a red tide doesn't last long. "Nature" has a way of correcting the balance. There are too many plankton, they begin to die out, and pretty soon everything is back to normal, including the color of the water.

But as the second angel pours out his bowl full of God's wrath in Revelation 16, I can imagine a red tide that grows and grows until it has covered all the oceans, leaving them stinking and polluted. There would be no fishing industry. You couldn't go into a restaurant and order lobster, shrimp, or crab legs. And you wouldn't find any health food restaurants advertising that they used "sea salt."

Just think of the havoc this would wreak on the world's economy.

It is also possible that the contamination of the earth's water will come about because of acid rain.

I remember, when I was a little boy, occasionally feeling depressed and cooped up on a rainy day—especially if that rainy day was a Saturday when I should have been outside playing. My mother always encouraged me by explaining that we needed the rain, and that it was bringing life to the earth. It was causing the grass, flowers, trees, and other plants to grow, and it was also giving us water to drink.

But today, in some parts of the United States and Canada, rain that falls into ponds and streams is not an unmitigated blessing. Its high acid content is actually killing fish and upsetting the ecological balance.

Acid rain has been the subject of a continuing debate between the U.S. and Canada, in fact, because the Canadian government wants tighter controls on American manufacturers whose smokestacks pour smoke and other pollutants into the atmosphere. These extra ingredients are included in the rain making process.

It would be bad enough if the acid rain fell right back over the area that produced it, but it doesn't. Instead, winds can blow the poisonous mix hundreds of miles from the point of origin. It's easy to see why the Canadian government is making noise! And only recently has the U.S. made serious overtures to Canada to resolve this problem.

It's also true, right now, that the problem is fairly confined to various regions—such as the Northeastern industrial corridor of the United States and Southeastern Canada. But, as I said before, one never knows where those atmospheric winds will be taking the acid rain mix, and the problem is not going to be alleviated anytime soon.

Too many businesses choose to maximize profits over any other consideration, including the safety of the public and the welfare of the planet. Am I pointing my finger at businessmen and accusing them of being particularly selfish? Of course not. I'm saying it's the nature of all human beings to be selfish, because we are all sinners. These businesses that seek to cut corners and throw pollutants into the earth's water and air are simply carrying out these "normal" human impulses on a much larger scale.

And so the angel has proclaimed rightly that God's judgments upon the earth are just. The people of earth will not only be getting the punishment they deserve, but the punishment they have brought on themselves.

Have you ever heard about something particularly terrible and asked yourself how God could allow this to happen?

Perhaps you've read about a drunk driver who lost control of his car and killed someone's son or daughter, or a depraved criminal who wiped out an entire family just to satisfy his blood lust. You've undoubtedly read accounts of the atrocities committed by the Khmer Rouge in Cambodia, Idi Amin in Uganda, and other savage regimes around the world. How can God be so patient?

Almost everyone has said, at one time or another, "If I were God, I'd make somebody pay for that!" It's a good thing that none of us is God, because we wouldn't give out many second chances. None of us could ever be as patient or as loving as the heavenly Father.

But now, after thousands of years of love, patience, and attempts to get people to change their ways, God will finally have had enough.

You almost get the sense that the angels will nudge one another and say, "It's about time, isn't it?" Angels are not born and they don't die. They were created by God in the same state in which they now exist. That means that for all the earth's history, they have been able to watch what has happened on this planet. And if we get sour stomachs over a few newspaper headlines, imagine how the angels must feel after witnessing thousands of years of wicked, cruel behavior.

But what did God do? Instead of destroying the entire human race with one snap of His fingers, He sent His own Son here to die in our behalf. Even now He has provided a way of escape, because anyone who turns to Him through accepting the sacrificial death of Jesus will be spared the calamities that are falling upon the earth.

But as judgment falls, the angel will not be able to contain himself. He says, in effect, "They have shed the blood of Your saints, and now You are making them drink blood. It's exactly what they deserve." (See Revelation 16:5–6.)

The Plague of the Sun

The fourth angel poured out his bowl on the sun, and the sun was given power to scorch people with fire. They were seared by the intense heat and they cursed the name of God, who had control over these plagues, but they refused to repent and glorify him.   Revelation 16:8–9

John may be describing a nova condition, in which a star begins to expand rapidly. This expansion may take anywhere from a day to a week, but suddenly the star is putting out vastly larger amounts of heat and light. Once the star has reached its maximum it begins to shrink, but normally it won't get back to its original size for twenty years or so.

Most scientists believe that a nova occurs when a star is collapsing because it has exhausted its supply of hydrogen, the basic fuel most stars, including our sun, burn. In other words, this condition is a star's "last gasp" as it nears the end of its life.

Scientists tell us that our sun will go on burning just as it does now for several billion more years—but they forget that time and the universe are both held in God's hands. As our planet nears the end of its life, it makes sense to think that the sun, moon, and other planets will also begin to crumble and die.

But maybe the scorching heat will not be caused so much by changes within the sun as by changes within the earth's atmosphere. We've already talked about holes in the ozone layer allowing more ultraviolet rays from the sun to reach the earth.

It could be that the ozone layer will come apart during this time, and that the earth will be bombarded by these dangerous rays.

It is also possible that the searing heat will come about through escalation of what scientists have in recent years begun to call "greenhouse effect, a process involving increasing atmospheric carbon dioxide." Year by year, scientists tell us, our planet is getting warmer.

This is cause for concern, because a continued warming trend would melt much of the polar icecaps, thus resulting in worldwide flooding as ocean levels rise. A warming trend would also cause the earth to lose more cropland, and we are already losing millions of acres to advancing deserts every year.

There are other vicious cycles that feed on themselves. As trees are cut down—for example, in vast sections of tropical rain forest—the desert advances and temperatures rise. As temperatures rise, vegetation that cannot withstand the increased heat dies out, and the desert advances some more.

This is a possible explanation for the increase in the earth's temperature as recorded by John here in the sixteenth chapter of Revelation.

Imagine a day in New York City or Chicago when the temperature has reached 115 or 120° F., and it's horribly humid, too. Imagine the violence that would occur as tempers escalate along with the temperature. Would people suffering from such heat turn to God and begin to glorify Him? More likely we'd hear a great deal of cursing and blaspheming the name of God, just as John describes here.

As I think about what is going to come upon this planet, I'm thankful God has promised that those who have kept His Word will be kept from the time of Tribulation.

A Time of Darkness

> The fifth angel poured out his bowl on the throne of the beast, and his kingdom was plunged into darkness. Men gnawed their tongues in agony and cursed the God of heaven because of their pains and their sores, but they refused to repent of what they had done.
>
> Revelation 16:10–11

If we read the account of the plagues that God, through Moses, brought upon the land of Egypt, we find that the ninth plague brought darkness over the entire country. Exodus 10:21–23 says:

> Then the Lord said to Moses, "Stretch out your hand toward the sky so that darkness will spread over Egypt— darkness that can be felt." So Moses stretched out his hand toward the sky, and total darkness covered all Egypt for three days. No one could see anyone else or leave his place for three days. Yet all the Israelites had light in the places where they lived.

Have you ever been driving along on a dark night when a thick fog suddenly rolls in, limiting your vision so that you can't even see the taillights of the car in front of you? This happens frequently along the coast of Southern California, and it can be terrifying.

You're driving along and everything's fine. It may be a bit foggy, but not enough to give you any problems. The next thing you know you're completely closed in. What do you do? If you keep going, hoping you'll come out the other side of the fog bank, you might hit someone. If you stop, someone might hit you. And if you try to pull off to the side of the road, you might wind up in a ditch.

Every so often I'll see a news article about a multiple car pileup caused by a blinding fog. When John talks about darkness covering the kingdom of the Beast, I picture it rolling in as heavy and thick as a Southern California fog. The darkness that will come upon the kingdom of the Beast may be caused by a combination of things. Because this plague follows closely on the heels of the plague in which the sun scorched people with its intense heat, it could be that the sun will have passed through the nova stage and begun to fade away to the point where it is now nothing more than a faintly glowing ember. In Matthew, recall that Jesus affirmed the prophecy of Joel that "the sun will be turned to darkness and the moon to blood before the coming of the great and dreadful day of the Lord" (Joel 2:31; see Matthew 24:29). That great and dreadful day is the day Jesus returns to establish God's Kingdom upon the earth.

Whatever causes it, the darkness will apparently be coupled with a disruption of electrical power and will bring on a time of terror, during which men will sit in the darkness and curse God.

Paving the Way for Armageddon

Next, the sixth bowl of God's wrath will be poured out upon

> the great river Euphrates, and its water was dried up to
> prepare the way for the kings from the East. Then I saw
> three evil spirits that looked like frogs; they came out of the
> mouth of the dragon, out of the mouth of the beast and out
> of the mouth of the false prophet. They are spirits of
> demons performing miraculous signs, and they go out to
> the kings of the whole world, to gather them for the battle
> on the great day of God Almighty.   Revelation 16:12–14

God is now beginning to gather armies from the nations of
the world into the Valley of Megiddo for the final confrontation
between His forces and the forces of Satan.

The leaders of the nations from the East—China, Japan,
India, Pakistan, Afghanistan, etc.—will begin advancing toward the Middle East. God will even have prepared the way for
their advance by seeing to it that the Euphrates River is dried
up.

This great river runs some 1,700 miles through the Middle
East. It ranges from three to twelve miles wide with an average
depth of thirty feet. At the present time Soviet engineers working in Syria are building a dam across this river. We are seeing
the beginnings of the fulfillment of this prophecy: When the
dam is completed the Euphrates River will never be the same.

And so the leaders from the East will move forward bent on
defeating God Himself, but it is they and their armies who will
be crushed.

As the last days arrive upon the planet, Satan will whisper
to those he has helped put into power and call them forward
to Armageddon, where he will ask them to help him prevent the
return of Christ. Those who listen are poor fools headed only
for their own destruction.

While the kings and their armies are gathering, Jesus is poised in the doorway, ready to make His triumphant return to the earth.

> "Behold, I come like a thief! Blessed is he who stays awake and keeps his clothes with him, so that he may not go naked and be shamefully exposed."   Revelation 16:15

It Is Finished

The time has come for the seventh and last of God's plagues to be poured out. And as the angel pours this final bowl into the air, there will be lightning and thunder and a loud voice crying out from the Temple, "It is done!"

When John heard this cry, I'm sure his mind went back to the day many years before when he stood before the cross of his Lord, Savior, and friend, Jesus Christ, and heard the same thing, "It is finished," as Jesus uttered His last words before He died.

What a difference in the meaning of those words! When Jesus said them on the cross, He meant that His mission was accomplished and that His life had been poured out as an atonement for any who would believe in Him.

But now those words mean that the evil world has run its course. God's patience has been exhausted and it is time for men to pay for their evil deeds.

When Jesus was on the cross the words *It is finished* opened the door for men and women everywhere to enter into eternal rest with Him. Now the words *It is done* shut the door and announce that the time of this opportunity has passed.

Following the sound of the voice, a severe earthquake will hit the planet. John says that no earthquake like this one has ever occurred before.

> The great city split into three parts, and the cities of the
> nations collapsed.   Revelation 16:19

I doubt if there is anything scarier than an earthquake. Those of us who live in California have become accustomed to the earth shaking beneath us—little tremors that wake us occasionally in the middle of the night or start the coffee sloshing around as we're having breakfast. Sometimes we may think, *Oh, an earthquake isn't really such a big deal.* Then a stronger quake hits and shows us that, yes, indeed, an earthquake really can be a big deal! When the ground beneath us begins to shake violently, our sense of security suddenly flees.

What could be more secure than the ground we walk on?—until it suddenly seems to turn into gelatin.

Imagine, then, what it will be like when the world is hit by a devastating quake that topples entire cities. This earthquake apparently won't be localized, either, but will travel the length and breadth of the earth.

Isaiah talked about the same thing when he wrote:

> The floodgates of the heavens are opened, the foundations
> of the earth shake. The earth is broken up, the earth is split
> asunder, the earth is thoroughly shaken. The earth reels
> like a drunkard, it sways like a hut in the wind; so heavy
> upon it is the guilt of its rebellion that it falls—never to
> rise again.
>   In that day the Lord will punish the powers in the
> heavens above and the kings on the earth below.
>   Isaiah 24:18–21

We don't know for sure what is going to cause the earthquake, but John says that the islands will flee and the mountains will not be found. We talked before about what would happen if a gigantic meteorite slammed into the earth and shifted our planet on its axis. This could be what John has witnessed here;

and if so, it could also be that the impact will knock the earth out of its usual orbit.

Something else comes to mind, too, when I think of Isaiah's prophecy that the world will "reel like a drunkard."

Scientists tell us that the earth wobbles about its axis as it travels around the sun. This "wobble effect" cycles every seven years. It starts with a very slight wobble, so minor as to be barely noticeable. But it continues to grow worse and worse until, seven years into the cycle, our planet is wobbling like a toy top about to wind down. Then the situation seems to correct itself, the wobble stops, and the cycle begins all over again.

Some scientists have suggested that there have been occasions in the earth's history when the wobble did not correct itself after seven years. Instead it became worse and worse, finally getting to the point where the earth just shifted on its axis. If and when this happened, islands would have sunk beneath the sea, mountains would have disappeared, cities would have collapsed, and there would have been general devastation everywhere.

When I was a boy, you used to be able to buy a wooden top at any toystore for a dime. You wound it up with string, and then you pulled the string as you threw the top to the sidewalk. If you got a good spin on it, you could watch it spin for two minutes or so. But no matter how good the spin, sooner or later as it began to slow down the top would start to wobble. The wobble would get worse and worse, until finally the top just fell over on its side. Watching a top wobble like that always put into my mind the picture of a drunk man staggering down the street on his way home from a bar.

That's why, when I remember Isaiah's words that the world will reel like a drunkard, I envision a spinning top beginning to wobble.

If this is what happens, and the planet is shifted on its axis, or if it is knocked out of its orbit after impact with a huge asteroid or meteorite, the planet's weather would change drastically, abruptly. This could help to explain the next part of John's vision:

> From the sky huge hailstones of about a hundred pounds each fell upon men. And they cursed God on account of the plague of hail, because the plague was so terrible.
>
> Revelation 16:21

You may remember that one of the plagues God brought upon Egypt was a severe hailstorm (Exodus 9:13–35). But it was nothing like the hail John has seen. I've heard of "Texas-sized" hail, and hail the size of golfballs, but it's hard for me to visualize the damage inflicted by hailstones weighing in the neighborhood of a hundred pounds each.

Yet John says that's what's coming.

I saw a news story not long ago about a huge chunk of ice that fell from the sky and smashed through someone's roof. Thankfully no one was injured, but the authorities were baffled as to where this block of ice—which weighed around 25 pounds—had come from. An investigation led to the conclusion that it fell from an airliner and that it was, in fact, water from an airplane toilet. How it escaped from the plane I have no idea—but the authorities say that's what happened.

Imagine what it would be like to have huge chunks of ice, four times the size of this, falling from the sky all around you. There would be no place to hide. These stones of ice would be falling through the roofs of buildings, smashing cars and trucks, causing entire buildings to collapse. The devastation would be incredible.

But this will be the last of God's judgments to fall upon the earth in general.

The time will have come to repay the great whore—Babylon the great—for her evil, and to end the Antichrist's reign of terror.

9
The Fall of Babylon

Revelation 17–19:4

> One of the seven angels who had the seven bowls came and
> said to me, "Come, I will show you the punishment of
> the great prostitute, who sits on many waters. With her
> the kings of the earth committed adultery and the inhabi-
> tants of the earth were intoxicated with the wine of her
> adulteries."   Revelation 17:1–2

After these words, John explains that he was carried away in
the spirit to a desert where he saw a woman sitting on a scarlet
Beast. This is the same Beast we met in chapter 13, because
John reminds us now that it has seven heads, ten horns, and is
covered with blasphemous names.

The woman is obviously some sort of royalty—or at least she
has set herself up as such. John says she is dressed in purple and
scarlet, and is covered with glittering gold, precious stones, and
pearls. She also holds a golden cup in her hand, which is "filled
with abominable things and the filth of her adulteries."

John also describes her as being "drunk with the blood of the
saints, the blood of those who bore testimony to Jesus," and as
having this title written on her forehead:

Mystery
Babylon the Great
The Mother of Prostitutes
And of the Abominations of the Earth.

The apostle John tells us that he was "greatly astonished" when he saw her, and no wonder. John's visions have included plenty of strange, hideous creatures and all sorts of wondrous happenings—but who is this regal woman who has drunk the blood of the saints?

In the next few verses of chapter 17, the angel tells John that he will explain who the woman is and what the vision signifies.

The problem for the average reader is that the angel's explanation raises as many questions as it answers!

"The beast, which you saw, once was, now is not, and will come up out of the Abyss and go to his destruction. The inhabitants of the earth whose names have not been written in the book of life from the creation of the world will be astonished when they see the beast, because he once was, now is not, and yet will come.

"This calls for a mind with wisdom. The seven heads are seven hills on which the woman sits. They are also seven kings. Five have fallen, one is, the other has not yet come; but when he does come, he must remain for a little while. The beast who once was, and now is not, is an eighth king. He belongs to the seven and is going to his destruction.

"The ten horns you saw are ten kings who have not yet received a kingdom, but who for one hour will receive authority as kings along with the beast. They have one purpose and will give their power and authority to the beast. They will make war against the Lamb, but the Lamb will overcome them because he is Lord of lords and King of kings—and with him will be his called, chosen and faithful followers."

Then the angel said to me, "The waters you saw, where the prostitute sits, are peoples, multitudes, nations and languages. The beast and the ten horns you saw will hate the prostitute. They will bring her to ruin and leave her

naked; they will eat her flesh and burn her with fire. For
God has put it into their hearts to accomplish his purpose
by agreeing to give the beast their power to rule, until
God's words are fulfilled. The woman you saw is the great
city that rules over the kings of the earth."

Revelation 17:8–18

John apparently understood everything the angel was telling
him, but those of us who are living 2,000 years later may need
to do some digging. Bear in mind, too, that John had to be very
careful in what he was writing. He could not always spell
everything out in plain language lest his book fall into the
wrong hands.

John didn't want this book to be seen by the Emperor Domitian, for instance, who was the head of the Roman Empire while
John was exiled on Patmos from 95–96 A.D. Domitian was
involved in bloody persecution of Christians, even as the apostle was having his vision of beasts, wicked kings, and bloody
prostitutes.

To say that Domitian wouldn't have been happy with John's
writing is an understatement. He was another in a line of
Roman emperors who hated Christians and had done everything in their power to rid the world of these "cultists." Domitian proclaimed himself to be of divine origin, and he could
tolerate no "competition" from other gods.

Meanwhile, Christians could still remember the bloody persecution unleashed by the Emperor Nero who ruled from 54–68
A.D. When Rome had suffered a disastrous fire during his reign,
Nero had blamed the Christians, though there wasn't the least
bit of evidence to back his assertions.

Never one to be stopped by a lack of evidence, Nero instituted mass executions in which hundreds—perhaps thousands—of believers were crucified.

When John writes about the king who is currently in power,
he is probably referring to Domitian. If the tyrannical emperor

had read this, and the part about another king to come, he would probably have gone on a bloody rampage. How dare John write these things about him! How dare John even suggest that there would be another king after him!

Domitian would have recognized the seven hills upon which the woman sits, just as you undoubtedly did, as the city of Rome. Because Rome was the capital of his kingdom, Domitian would have taken further offense at this book and assumed it was all about him. The truth is, despite the fact that he was such a bloody character, he is referred to only in passing.

Meanwhile, the Christians who were living during the reign of Domitian were growing impatient, wondering when Jesus was going to return and make things right. When was all the persecution going to end? They knew God had said, "Vengeance is mine," but they were ready now for Him to act.

John wanted them to know that God was going to move decisively, but the time had not yet come. The duty of believers is to trust in God, to suffer for Him if need be, and to know that the joys that await them in His Kingdom will make their present difficulties seem like nothing.

But John was not concerned so much in chapter 17 with the things that are happening in the kingdoms of the earth. His main concern here—or rather, the concern of the angel who showed him the vision—is the corruption of the Church from within.

God's Church has always been able to stand strong in the face of opposition from without—whether in ancient Rome, modern Russia, or anywhere else. The real danger comes when she begins to replace God's rules with her own manmade traditions.

This "whore of Babylon," then, is a false religious system that has trapped the souls of men—a religious system that is in Revelation 17 about to fall.

To discover who this woman is, we need to think about the origins of Babylon itself.

The Origins of Babylon

Babylon is used in the Scriptures as a symbol of confusion. After all, it was in Babylon (or Babel) where man, in rebellion against God, decided to build a tower whereby he could "reach into heaven." (The story is recorded in Genesis 11.)

It is my belief that ancient man was not as primitive and ignorant as we picture him. There are indications that the people of that day had tremendous means of communication—perhaps even superior in some ways to our own. I think they understood the communications potential of crystal, for example, and may have incorporated this in "communications centers" such as England's Stonehenge. It's a distinct possibility that they had set up such centers to communicate with beings from beyond the earth.

With whom were they communicating? The Bible does not say specifically that God did *not* create other beings that live on other planets, so that is one possibility. I think it is more likely, however, that they were seeking wisdom from demons masquerading as wise and benevolent beings.

In Babylon, man decided he was going to build the greatest communications center ever. A huge tower that would reach into the heavens, it would put all the wisdom and power of the universe at his disposal.

But the Bible says God looked down from heaven and saw what man was doing. At this time, everyone on earth spoke the same language. There were no communication problems, no ethnic or racial barriers. The human race was one large, cooperative family. And God saw that this unity was being used for evil rather than for good.

The unity had to be broken, so He supernaturally gave people different languages. Suddenly people couldn't understand what others were saying. Can you imagine how frustrating it must have been to be conversing with a friend only to have him suddenly start acting as if he didn't have the slightest idea what you were talking about? At first you'd think he was kidding, but as time went on you'd begin to see that he really couldn't understand you—because when he tried to talk to you, you'd think *he* had gone completely nuts.

And then a third friend came along, and neither one of you could understand him. What a day that must have been!

And so the Tower of Babel, intended to be man's greatest achievement and a reflection of the unity of the human race, became instead the symbol of confusion and disarray. Today if someone is speaking in a language we don't understand, or just talking nonsense, we say that he's babbling. This illustrates how the name *Babylon* has come to be synonymous with confusion and unintelligible sounds.

What does this have to do with the prostitute riding on the back of the Beast?

She signifies the confusion and disorder that have crept into the Church. God presented a simple plan whereby man could be forgiven of his sins and brought into a right relationship with God. It's not an *easy* plan, because it involved the death of God's only Son, but it is *simple* in that it requires nothing more than that a man believe in Christ and accept what He has done.

When Christ died, the veil in the Temple was torn in two, signifying that through Christ man was now able to come directly into the presence of God. He didn't need any other mediator but Christ, nor did he need a succession of priests, saints, angels, or any other creatures to stand between him and God.

As far as God is concerned, all Christians are equal. There is no ranking or bureaucracy in His Church, and no room for certain men lording it over others and thinking themselves to be closer to God or more worthy of His grace.

God set up His perfect order. But then man came along and wrapped it up in a big ball of confusion.

As the Church's structure grew over the years after Christ's death, it became more and more bureaucratic. Men began to vie for offices within the Church, not because they wanted to be servants of God's people, but because they wanted the power and the prestige it brought them. They wanted to wear fancy robes, have others call them by long titles, and enjoy the respect of the communities in which they lived.

More confusion resulted when, as the Gospel was taken to primitive peoples, many of their religious customs were taken into the Church. Accepting these pagan practices in an effort to make it easier for these people to accept Christ, and covering them with a veneer of Christianity, only perverted and complicated God's simple plan.

The whore of Babylon, then, was she who pretended to be God's Church, perhaps even truthfully thought of herself as such, but was in reality nothing of the sort. Instead she persecuted those who truly stood for God—imprisoning them, burning them at the stake, drowning them—just as the Israelites had often reacted with brutal hatred toward the prophets God sent to them. (In this regard *Foxe's Book of Martyrs* is a real eye-opener!)

The whore of Babylon has brought man to the place where he no longer trusts in the blood of Christ to save him. Instead, he trusts in rituals or in his own goodness.

The whore of Babylon also brings superstition into God's Church, convincing people not to put their faith in Christ, but to invest it instead in medals, statues, and patron saints.

The relationship between the erring Church and the ancient kingdom of Babylon is more than a spiritual one. She has even incorporated into her life, as we have already seen, several practices that originated in the land of Babylon.

For instance, the ancient Babylonians worshiped a god called Nimrod, also known as Tammuz. The Bible speaks about Nimrod, telling us in Genesis 10:8–12 that he was a mighty hunter and a great king, a grandson or great-grandson of Noah. He was an ordinary human being. But in Babylon, his legend grew to the point that he was considered to be a god.

The Babylonians actually believed he was born of a virgin. It was said that while he was hunting he was gored by a wild boar and died. His body lay in state for three days, after which he was resurrected.

Also woven into the worship of Nimrod was a great deal of emphasis on fertility. And so to celebrate his "resurrection," the Babylonians would color eggs—a symbol of fertility—and give them to one another. They also began to include images of rabbits—noted, of course, for their fertility—in their worship rites.

The main reason for the emphasis on fertility was that Nimrod's mother, Astarte, was considered to be the goddess of fertility, so the celebration of her son's resurrection bore her name. We can see that it's not too big a leap from *Astarte* to *Easter*.

If that's not enough to show how Babylonian superstitions have crept into the Church, there's more.

Beyond being resurrected, it was also said that Nimrod was born on December 25. And guess what the Babylonians did to celebrate his birthday? They went into the forest, cut down trees, brought them into their houses, and decorated them with gold and silver. Not just any tree would do. It had to be an evergreen, considered by the Babylonians to be the symbol of sustained life.

Are all these things a matter of coincidence? That seems highly unlikely.

One may be tempted to ask how the story of Nimrod could so closely parallel the life of Christ. Satan apparently had some sort of knowledge, albeit imperfect, of God's plan to save the world through His Son, and he sought to counterfeit God's plan. Did Nimrod actually die and come back to life three days later? Of course not. But if Satan could get people to believe that about Nimrod, they would be less inclined to see the uniqueness of Christ, and to understand that He and He alone was God's

Son, the way to salvation. Satan, as we've already seen, is a master counterfeiter.

How did all of these Babylonian practices—the Easter bunny, the colored eggs, the decorating of trees—find their way into the Church? Through Satan, who sought to deceive God's people and keep them enslaved to pagan customs and superstitions.

I am sure many readers won't like what I'm saying, and will wonder if I'm trying to be some sort of spoilsport. "What are you trying to do—steal Christmas and Easter from us?"

No, I'm simply telling the truth, and showing how we may inadvertently be bowing the knee to ancient satanic gods without even being aware of what we are doing. Let us take great care, as I said earlier, to keep our focus on Jesus Christ during our celebration of these holidays, and set them apart as true "holy days" unto the Lord.

We see, then, that the woman who rides on the Beast is false religion masquerading as the true Church of Christ. If you are interested in more documented information on this subject, I refer you to the book *The Two Babylons* by Alexander Hislop (Loizeaux).

Now what about the Beast who "once was, now is not, and will come up out of the Abyss"?

This appears to be one of the five previous Roman emperors who had ruled prior to the time John was writing the book of Revelation. He was gone from the scene now as John was writing, but he would return to the world in some form during the reign of the Antichrist in the final days.

Of all the Roman emperors, the one who fits this description best is Caesar Nero. In Hebrew, in fact, Nero's name numerically totals 666, and this madman was known as "the beast" by the Christians who lived during his reign.

Anyone who studies the life of Nero has to come to one of two conclusions: Either he was totally crazy or he was possessed by evil spirits. There is no other way to explain the terrible things he did. Considering the way he raged against the Christian Church, he must have been influenced by demons.

When Nero first became emperor, he seemed to be a fairly decent fellow, as emperors went. But something happened that turned him into a raving lunatic. Interestingly enough, it seems that a drastic change occurred in his life shortly after the apostle Paul stood before him and preached the Gospel. (You may remember from the book of Acts how Paul was sent to plead his case before Caesar. See Acts 25:12.) Nero was in power at this time, and Paul undoubtedly attempted to convince him to become a Christian, even as he did with King Agrippa. In refusing to accept the Lord, Nero may have opened himself up to demonic influence.

In any case, he launched a terrible wave of persecution, and was responsible for the deaths of thousands of Christians. He actually set believers on fire and used them to light his garden. Then he would drive his chariot in and out among their burning bodies, shrieking with glee. He originally set Paul free, but had him rearrested and brought back to Rome, where he had the apostle beheaded. He also condemned Peter to death and had him crucified upside-down.

My belief is that the same demon or demons that possessed the Emperor Nero will possess the Antichrist. Just as Nero showed himself publicly as a man of refined tastes, someone who loved the arts and music, but underneath was a scheming, horrible, blood-thirsty man, so the Antichrist will show himself as a noble champion of the people even while he plots to destroy them.

When this demonic monster returns to the world's stage, he won't have mellowed a great deal over the last 2,000 years.

Could it be that Nero himself will be returning to the scene as well? I don't know. But just imagine all the evil geniuses from throughout earth's history whom Satan now has at his command. Certainly Satan will use them as he leads the armies of hell in a final, desperate assault on God. These are men who will know they have nothing to lose. God has already condemned them for all eternity. Their only chance will be to overthrow God's Kingdom and establish their own eternal kingdom of darkness and horror.

They will be joined in their fight by the ten kings who will receive authority along with the Beast.

Once again, there has been a great deal of speculation over the years as to the identity of these ten kings, but all the evidence suggests they will be the rulers of the nations that make up the European Community. I believe this makes sense. There are a fluctuating number of nations in this economic "United States of Europe," but the number hovers around ten. Furthermore, as I write this book, the member nations are moving toward a unified economy.

Since current plans call for the virtual removal of all government borders by the end of 1992, and a single monetary system, the idea is to shape Western Europe into a first-class economic power. I'm not saying that the nations will dissolve into one super-nation, but there is obvious strength in unity and in numbers.

The growing strength of the European Community increases the likelihood of a strong, centralized government—and also makes it possible for one man to assume power over all the nations. This is a federation of strong nations and weak nations—of iron and clay as in Nebuchadnezzar's dream in Daniel 2.

Europe: Ripe for Plucking

If you travel through Western Europe today, you step into a post-Christian world and get a sense that the continent is ripe for plucking by the Antichrist. Moral decay has increased as the Christian Church has lost its influence. People are either apathetic or openly engaged in depravity. Look into their eyes and you can see the hopelessness and despair.

I'm not saying that all of Europe is this way—but the signs of religious decay are well in evidence.

It's strange but true that in Eastern Europe, where the Church is being persecuted, we find revivals breaking out everywhere. People are losing their jobs or going to jail because they want to serve the Lord. In Western Europe, by contrast, where there is no organized opposition to the Church, it's hard to find many who care enough to attend church on Sunday.

The younger residents of Western Europe seem especially apathetic. They have rejected the truth, have nothing else to believe in, and nothing to get excited about. But when the Antichrist comes along, he will fill that void in their lives, getting them fired up over his own aims and programs.

Those who reject the truth are bound to believe a lie, and so the Antichrist's rise to power will be greatly aided by current conditions in Europe.

The Beast vs. the Prostitute

In verse 16 of the seventeenth chapter, John says that the Beast and the ten kings will hate the prostitute and will bring her to ruin.

This is hard to understand, since the prostitute, the Beast, and the ten kings all seem to be on the same side. Their motives are to destroy men and to lead them away from God, aren't they?

The answer is no. The prostitute, the false church that reaches out through all the world from her base in Rome, proclaims and perhaps even believes that she is serving God, although she has wandered far from His plan and purposes. The Antichrist and his closest followers are under no such illusions. They know they are serving Satan and they serve him gladly in exchange for earthly power.

Is the prostitute the Roman Catholic Church? After all, the prostitute has brought Babylonian practices into God's Church—just as the Catholic Church has done in many ways—and both are headquartered at Rome.

I personally know many Roman Catholics who are fine Christians and who serve the Lord with zeal. But remember, by the time the Antichrist begins his dealings with the great prostitute, all who belonged to God's true Church will have been raptured from the earth. Millions will come to know the Lord after the Rapture has taken place, but these people will not be part of the Church. The age of the Church will have passed, and any organized denominational structures that remain behind will be nothing but empty shells.

It is true, in the meantime, that the Catholic Church has taken many steps away from God. Roman Catholicism teaches, for instance, that we cannot be saved without receiving the sacraments, whereas the Bible clearly teaches that we are saved through faith in Christ alone. She teaches that we can pray to the saints, while the Bible says there is only one Mediator between God and man, the Lord Jesus Christ. The Roman Catholic Church has brought into her life a number of such teachings that are simply not biblical and not ordained of God. Far from bringing people closer to God, they make Him seem more distant and unattainable. But is this the doing of the Roman Catholic Church alone? Obviously not. If we look at some of today's Protestant denominations, we see many churches that have gone full-speed-ahead into error. These are churches that seem to have forgotten all about Jesus Christ, in which you could sit Sunday after Sunday and never hear His name mentioned.

A friend told me how startled he was to talk with a Presbyterian pastor who admitted, "I'm not really sure what I believe. I suppose I'm an agnostic."

"An agnostic?" my friend said. "What do you tell your people when you preach to them?"

"Oh, I tell them to keep a positive outlook. To try to be happy. To be good to each other."

My friend went away shaking his head, wondering what sort of comfort this man could bring to a bereaved family. He had nothing to offer the members of his congregation but cold, joyless humanism.

It's hard for me to imagine why a man who didn't believe in God would want to be in the ministry at all! The fact that this man was ordained by one of the Presbyterian denominations is not intended as a slam. It only shows that error and unbelief cut across denominational lines. A close look at dozens of Protestant denominations will reveal many that corrupt the simple Gospel message, adding thick layers of man's teaching.

Whenever this has happened, it is as if the Church, which is the Bride of Christ, has forsaken her first love and gone after new lovers. She may believe she is being faithful to Him, but she has allowed so many idols to come between Him and her that she can barely remember what He looks like.

It is noteworthy that when Jesus was addressing the seven churches, He had many good things to say about Thyatira, which represents Roman Catholicism in church history; yet He did not have one good thing to say about Sardis, representing dead Protestantism, which had a name of being alive but in reality was dead.

Protestant churches don't pledge allegiance to the Pope, but many are linked to the prostitute by their actions.

As I write this, there is a reform movement afoot within the Catholic Church that is gaining steam. There are those who realize that some of the Church's current teachings are not biblical, that they make the sacrifice of Jesus less than pivotal. They understand that man is saved by Jesus alone, and not Jesus plus anything else.

So far the Church seems for the most part to be welcoming these reforms with open arms. Will she continue to do so?

I believe there will be a sharp polarization in the future.

Those who love God and want to serve Him will move ahead with the reforms. On the other side of the battle will be those who love the Church more than they love Christ. Their desire will be to preserve the traditions, the Babylonian mystery with its pomp and circumstance.

As this battle becomes more clearly defined, there will occur a division. One group will move ahead with Christ. The other group will stay behind without Him. One group will be going up in the Rapture. The other group won't. And so the great prostitute symbolizes the Church that has gone into error, *wherever that Church may be, whatever denominational (or non-denominational) name she hangs above the entrance to her buildings.*

What about the question as to why the Beast and his ten kings would hate the woman and want to destroy her? There are really two answers. First, they hate her because she is in many ways a reminder of Christ and His victory over them, and they hate anything in the least way connected to Him. Second, they hate her because she is powerful and therefore their rival. There are no loyalties in Satan's kingdom; it's every demon for himself in the grab for power.

While the Antichrist and his flunkies will hate the prostitute, they will also realize they can use her. So there will be an attempted alliance. You may remember how we talked about Christ's message to the church at Pergamum. This church had joined forces with the world's political systems. Co-opted by the state, its true power and authority were lost, and so was any ability to be a prophetic voice. How can you speak out against a government's wrong actions when you're part of that government?

That's what's going to happen here. The Antichrist will reach out with open arms to this great prostitute of a "Church," pledging his support to her and thereby hoping to win the allegiance of her millions of followers.

Do you remember what he is going to do in Jerusalem, where

he will help to rebuild the Temple and declare his friendship for the Jewish people, only to turn around and unleash a furious persecution against them?

He will do the same thing with the great prostitute. He will make friends with her, probably appointing many bishops and other church dignitaries to high governmental posts in his regime. They will be seduced by his promises of power and his apparent willingness to bring "the Church" into the decision-making process. "He cares about our concerns," they will say. In fact, he cares about nothing except power, and his friendship with the whoring "Church" will last only as long as it is useful to him.

This sort of thing has happened before, often in Communist or Marxist revolutions. When they are seeking to gain power, the revolutionaries make every effort to prove they are not opposed to religion. In Nicaragua, for instance, we saw many priests and other churchmen among the ranks of the rebellious armies that drove Anastasio Somoza from power. Once the Sandinista regime was firmly entrenched, however, religious freedoms were curtailed and priests' sermons were censored. The Church is now tolerated only as it acts in ways that benefit the government.

This is a model for what will happen under the Antichrist, except that persecution under him will make the persecution that has occurred under the Communists seem like nothing at all.

He will use this "Church" for anything he can get out of her, and then turn against her with a terrible vengeance: "They will bring her to ruin and leave her naked; they will eat her flesh and burn her with fire."

But as they do so, they will be accomplishing the purposes of God, who is sending His judgment upon this unfaithful bride.

And so spiritual Babylon has fallen.

The Second Babylon Falls

In the eighteenth chapter of Revelation, John turns his attention from spiritual Babylon to another type of Babylon—a Babylon of economic power that must also fall before God's judgment.

As the chapter opens, John tells us about another angel coming down from heaven with "great authority":

> With a mighty voice he shouted: "Fallen! Fallen is Babylon the Great! She has become a home for demons and a haunt for every evil spirit, a haunt for every unclean and detestable bird. For all the nations have drunk the maddening wine of her adulteries. The kings of the earth committed adultery with her, and the merchants of the earth grew rich from her excessive luxuries."
>
> Revelation 18:2–3

Then another voice from heaven calls God's people to

> "Come out of her . . . so that you will not share in her sins, so that you will not receive any of her plagues; for her sins are piled up to heaven, and God has remembered her crimes."
>
> Revelation 18:4–5

In verse 8 John records the voice as saying that this Babylon "will be consumed by fire, for mighty is the Lord God who judges her." Two verses later he tells us that the kings who dealt with Babylon will stand afar off as they see her burning and cry, "Woe! Woe, O great city, O Babylon, city of power! In one hour your doom has come!"

Who or what is this "commercial Babylon"? You may have

heard that she is the United States. Others say she is the Soviet Union or another of the world's current powers. Perhaps this new Babylon will stand in the rich, oil-producing region of the Middle East.

Over the last fifteen years or so, we have seen a tremendous shift in the world's economy. The nations of the Middle East have become richer and richer at the expense of the Western nations.

Most of us can remember how it was in 1973, when oil shortages first began to occur and life at the neighborhood gas station changed drastically overnight. Remember how we used to get a steak knife or a drinking glass every time we put gas in our cars? Service stations were just that—service stations. The attendant would wash the windshield, check the oil, check the air in our tires, and bring Green Stamps with our change.

Then everything changed. Suddenly lines at the station were twenty and thirty cars long and we were lucky if there was any gasoline left by the time we pulled up to the pump to get our rationed amount. For the most part the service was gone. So were the Green Stamps and free gifts.

Gasoline prices jumped dramatically, and even though the shortage didn't last all that long, the prices didn't come back down. In the late '70s, history repeated itself and gasoline prices climbed to the point where it wasn't unusual to be paying $1.40 or more a gallon.

What was going on? Simply a reaction to the fact that oil-producing nations had finally figured out they had the rest of the world over a barrel, so to speak. They knew we were dependent on their oil. They also knew we could talk all we wanted about developing alternative forms of energy, but we weren't very likely to do it. They had something the Western nations urgently needed, and there was no reason they shouldn't get a "fair" price for it.

Of course, they were right in their assessment of the situation.

And they were merely playing by the rules of free enterprise, which dictate that price is determined by supply and demand. If there is a small supply and a large demand, the price will be high.

Ever since the '70s there has been fluctuation in oil prices. They haven't stayed as high as they were, but they haven't come down all that much, either. More importantly, the oil producers have become much more involved in other areas of the world's economy. They have realized they cannot build lasting wealth and security on a one-product economy, so they have begun to diversify far beyond the production of oil.

Here in the United States, Middle Eastern concerns are buying or investing heavily in all sorts of businesses. Arab businessmen have purchased hotels, department stores, amusement parks, thousands of square miles of real estate, banks, and savings and loan institutions.

Since World War II, we have seen Japan come back after defeat to become one of the world's strongest economic powers. I believe that we will see an economic turnaround of even greater proportions in the Middle East.

Wherever the new Babylon is, whether in the Middle East or elsewhere, she will be a symbol of man's greed and determination to choose the material over the spiritual. Although there are differences of opinion regarding who she might be, there can be no argument that destruction will come upon her swiftly.

Why is God so strong in His condemnation of this new economic power? Because she will seduce the nations away from Him, using her economic power to bend other nations to her will.

Imagine, for instance, how a Middle Eastern Babylon would be able to use the lure of her oil to turn other nations against Israel. The implication would be, "If you are a friend of Israel you cannot be a friend of ours, and therefore cannot purchase our oil." This tactic could leave Israel isolated and estranged.

This new Babylon could help to bring about the invasion of
Israel by the kings from the East, which will precipitate
Armageddon.

In some Muslim countries, such as Egypt, it is already considered a capital offense to convert from Islam. It is possible
that a bloody wave of anti-Christian actions will take place
within this new economic power. It may become a capital offense to teach anyone about Christ, and I can foresee Christian
missionaries being imprisoned or even executed. Proselytizing
is already a crime in some countries; in Greece two missionaries
and a Greek pastor were convicted on that charge (though
finally acquitted) because they gave a New Testament to a
sixteen-year-old boy. The new Babylon is going to carry anti-
Christian fervor to new extremes, but God will not tolerate this
for long.

It could be that an all-out nuclear exchange will utterly
destroy her in one hour's time, just as the voice from heaven
said would happen. This especially makes sense in light of the
fact that those who once dealt with her—the leaders of allied
nations, the merchants, the sea captains who sailed in and out
of her ports—will stand afar off and watch her burn. The implication is that they don't want to get too close to her since that
could endanger their lives. Are they perhaps afraid of the nuclear fallout?

> Then a mighty angel picked up a boulder the size of a large
> millstone and threw it into the sea, and said: "With such
> violence the great city of Babylon will be thrown down,
> never to be found again. The music of harpists and musi-
> cians, flute players and trumpeters, will never be heard in
> you again. No workman of any trade will ever be found
> in you again. The sound of a millstone will never be heard
> in you again. The light of a lamp will never shine in you
> again. The voice of bridegroom and bride will never be
> heard in you again. Your merchants were the world's

great men. By your magic spell all the nations were led astray. In her was found the blood of prophets and of the saints, and of all who have been killed on the earth."

Revelation 18:21–24

Verse 23 in which the angel proclaims that Babylon's "magic spell" has led the nations astray is particularly interesting to me. It would seem to imply a worldwide blitz of advertising and public relations efforts in her behalf.

We've already heard of entire countries asking advertising agencies to help give them a better image, and sometimes it seems Madison Avenue could sell just about anything to just about anybody. And so, through the "magic" of advertising and imaging specialists, this new-age Babylon will be envied and admired throughout the entire world.

And then God will destroy her.

During her brief period of glory, she has stood for everything to which God is opposed. No wonder heaven rejoices over her destruction. In Revelation 19:1–2, we read:

> After this I heard what sounded like the roar of a great multitude in heaven shouting:
> "Hallelujah! Salvation and glory and power belong to our God, for true and just are his judgments. He has condemned the great prostitute who corrupted the earth by her adulteries. He has avenged on her the blood of his servants."

And so God will judge the false religious system that corrupted the earth with her spiritual fornication, and He will also condemn the economic Babylon that blinded the eyes of the world with her riches and fought so hard against the Lord.

And now the final curtain is about to descend upon a rebellious planet.

10

The Final Battle

The scene on earth is one of chaos and confusion. The great city of Babylon has fallen, dealing the earth's economy a blow from which she will be unable to recover. The Antichrist's throne is shaken and he struggles to hold on against increasingly loud voices of doubt and rebellion. He is pressed on all sides by those who would take his place, and as a result he will unleash a campaign of violent persecution.

In heaven, the scene is one of rejoicing and triumph. The judgments of God are true and just, and He has handed out punishments that have been long overdue. Heaven's joy is not brought about by the shedding of innocent blood, because no innocent blood has been shed.

There is also rejoicing in heaven because the angels know the time is drawing near for the Marriage Supper of the Lamb. The time has come for the Bridegroom, Jesus Christ, to be united with His Bride, the Church. This is a moment that has long been anticipated by all creation. The curtain is about to go up on the Millennium.

Christ's Bride, John says, has made herself ready, and has been given "fine linen, bright and clean." This signifies that she will be standing before Him in purity and righteousness.

This is not a righteousness based on good deeds she has done or medals and badges she has earned. Instead, she is made righteous through her faith in Jesus Christ.

Some people have what might be called a "brick wall" theology. They believe their salvation is secure as long as they're doing everything God expects of them—reading the Bible, witnessing to their friends, spending time in prayer, attending every church service, and so on. But suppose a day comes along in which they don't read the Bible or pray or witness to anyone—and perhaps they've been in a particularly surly mood, or even entertained an impure thought or two.

Then, on the way home from work, their car goes out of control and smashes into a brick wall, leaving them fatally injured.

Well, too bad, for now by their own theology they would likely not make it into heaven. With "brick wall" theology my salvation depends upon what I have done, and my own efforts bring me righteousness. Friends, this mindset has no biblical basis.

We all have bad days in which we don't live the way God expects us to. But that has no bearing on our salvation, because we are made righteous in God's eyes through faith in His Son—nothing more and nothing less. To think that our salvation is dependent on our own efforts is to minimize the work of Christ on the cross.

And so the Church, as she stands before her Husband-to-be, will be dressed in the purest, finest garments.

I can think of few experiences more thrilling than the wedding of two fine Christian people. It's such a joyful occasion to see God bring two people together, and to know they are going to establish a home and family centered around Jesus Christ. It's an especially exciting moment when the organist begins to play "The Wedding March," signaling that the bride is about to make her entrance.

All eyes turn toward the back of the church, and here she comes—in a beautiful gown with the train flowing behind her. A huge smile is on her face and love shines in her eyes. It's a stirring, emotional moment, and I would go so far as to say that

I've never seen a bride who wasn't beautiful.

But all that is only a tiny foretaste of what it will be like when the Bride of Christ walks down the aisle to meet Him at the altar.

John tells us he was so overwhelmed by the angel talking to him about these things that he fell at his feet to worship him. But the angel stopped him, saying: "Do not do it! I am a fellow servant with you and with your brothers who hold to the testimony of Jesus. Worship God! For the testimony of Jesus is the spirit of prophecy" (Revelation 19:10).

It is a common thing for men to begin to worship the instrument God has used to speak to us, rather than God Himself. Believers who have been given the gift of prophecy or healing or some other especially "exciting" spiritual gift have sometimes drawn attention to themselves and away from God. Or the emphasis may be placed on the gift itself, rather than on the One who gave it. I have known people seeking desperately after spiritual gifts who weren't all that interested in seeking after God. Whenever the Holy Spirit speaks, He exalts Jesus Christ.

Man has made the same mistake for thousands of years: He has seen the works of God and is attracted to those more than to the One behind the works. He is thrilled by the beauty of the creation, but fails to see the glory of the One who designed it. He is so impressed by the gift of healing at work that he fails to see the hand of God.

What did the angel mean when he said, "The testimony of Jesus is the spirit of prophecy"?

He meant that all prophecy centers around the Person of Jesus Christ. All the prophecies of the Old Testament centered around Him, pointed the way to Him, and foretold His coming. Since Jesus' death, burial, and resurrection, all prophecy has pointed people to Jesus, acknowledging that He is the only way of salvation, and that He is coming again.

Some people treat prophecy as if it were just another form of fortune-telling. But the Lord is less interested in telling you where you should invest your money or who you should marry than in pointing people to Jesus. In churches where "prophecy" is abused as fortune-telling, we're getting away from what God intended and taking a step toward becoming like the Babylonian church. She added extra steps between man and God— similar to this step of letting a "prophet" tell us what God wants us to do.

We must remember that "the testimony of Jesus is the spirit of prophecy."

The Army in the Sky

And now as John looks toward heaven he sees a breathtaking sight, for the King of kings, riding a dazzlingly white horse, is coming out of the sky. Behind Him rides His army dressed in sparkling white, also riding white horses.

This is indeed a thrilling moment. God has given Satan's followers every chance to turn away from their evil deeds and come to Him, but now His patience is exhausted and the time of battle has come.

And just who is in this army? You are! I am! Everyone who was raptured with the Church! What a tremendous privilege it will be to serve in the Lord's army.

John records the scene this way in Revelation 19:11–16:

> I saw heaven standing open and there before me was a white horse, whose rider is called Faithful and True. With justice he judges and makes war. His eyes are like blazing fire, and on his head are many crowns. He has a name written on him that no one knows but he himself. He is dressed in a robe dipped in blood, and his name is the Word of God. The armies of heaven were following him, riding on white horses and dressed in fine linen, white and clean. Out of his mouth comes a sharp sword with which

to strike down the nations. "He will rule them with an iron scepter." He treads the winepress of the fury of the wrath of God Almighty. On his robe and on his thigh he has this name written: KING OF KINGS AND LORD OF LORDS.

If we go back and look at the first three verses of the Gospel of John, we find these words:

"In the beginning was the Word, and the Word was with God, and the Word was God. He was with God in the beginning. Through him all things were made; without him nothing was made that has been made."

John has a unique understanding of Jesus Christ as the Word of God, and that is how he describes Him at this time.

What does John mean when he says that Jesus has a name written on Him "that no one but he himself knows"? This apparently means that Christ's nature is incomprehensible to human beings. He is fully God and yet He is fully man. How can we hope to understand this? For centuries, Church leaders have argued over the issue, trying to sort out His humanity and His divinity. Was He fully God at some times and fully human at others? The answer is that He is fully both at all times. We can't understand how this is possible, but we accept it by faith. And only Christ Himself knows how it can be true.

When John writes that Christ's garments will have been dipped in blood, he apparently means blood from the enemies of God and not the blood that Christ shed upon the cross for our salvation. For a parallel passage, we must turn once again to Isaiah 63, where we read in verses 1–4:

Who is this coming from Edom, from Bozrah, with his garments stained crimson?

Who is this, robed in splendor, striding forward in the greatness of his strength?

"It is I, speaking in righteousness, mighty to save."

Why are your garments red, like those of one treading
the winepress?

"I have trodden the winepress alone; from the nations
no one was with me. I trampled them in my anger and trod
them down in my wrath; their blood spattered my garments, and I stained all my clothing. For the day of vengeance was in my heart, and the year of my redemption
has come."

In the early days of wine-making, grapes were harvested and
place in huge vats. Then people climbed into the vats and
smashed the grapes with their feet, turning the task into a party
with everyone dancing on grapes. Imagine how their clothes
looked at the end of the day!

This is the second time John tells of Jesus trampling the
enemies of God as if they were so many grapes. It is another
way of saying that they will be utterly destroyed.

Meanwhile, all the armies loyal to the Antichrist will have
gathered themselves together to prevent Christ's return. They
will actually believe they have a chance to overcome God Himself. But how will God see them? Like so many fat grapes
waiting to be trampled.

There will be millions of soldiers from the Antichrist's armies
gathered in the Middle East. There will be tanks and trucks and
weapons of every type imaginable—a gathering of firepower so
great that all the wars in human history will seem like mere
rehearsals for this, the real thing.

From all over the world, the Antichrist's troops will come
pouring into the Middle East. Sophisticated tanks capable of
firing nuclear weapons will form row after row. Lines of infan-
trymen and mounted soldiers will continue for miles and miles,
marching along with the latest in heavy artillery. Fighter planes
will roar across the sky, soaring in tight formation, searching
for the enemy.

It will be the greatest display of unity the world has ever seen as the flags of dozens of nations fly together, all of them subordinate to the flag of the Antichrist—the great world ruler.

Where is the enemy? Who is the enemy? Who knows? But the Antichrist will have called, and his soldiers will have come ready to crush whoever stands in his way. Remember how the generals under Hitler later tried to excuse the atrocities they had committed by saying they were merely "following orders"? Some of the Antichrist's soldiers will serve him gladly, knowing exactly who he is and what he stands for. Others will be merely "following orders." Yet they, too, will have made their choice. They will have rejected the God of heaven and chosen a new god.

They will do anything he asks of them, whether it be murdering innocent men, women, and children, attacking defenseless cities with nuclear weapons, or coming to the Middle East to crush what they will probably see as a rebellion against their mighty champion.

But they won't realize that all this display of man's might is no match for the armies of God.

> And I saw an angel standing in the sun, who cried in a loud voice to all the birds flying in midair, "Come, gather together for the great supper of God, so that you may eat the flesh of kings, generals, and mighty men, of horses and their riders, and the flesh of all people, free and slave, small and great."   Revelation 19:17–18

The prophecy of David as recorded in the second psalm will be coming to pass: "Why do the nations conspire and the peoples plot in vain? The kings of the earth take their stand and the rulers gather together against the Lord and against his Anointed One. 'Let us break their chains,' they say, 'and throw off their fetters.' The One enthroned in heaven laughs; the Lord scoffs at them. Then he rebukes them in his anger and terrifies them in his wrath . . ." (Psalm 2:1–5).

We look at these people and think, *How foolish they are to think they can fight against God.*

But the truth is, there are many people in the world today who fight against God. We ourselves fight against Him when we know what He wants us to do and refuse to do it.

"Oh, I know God expects me to give to support His work, but I really need this new VCR."

"Yes, I know I need to be in church on Sunday morning, but it's the only day of the week I get to sleep in."

"I know the Bible says that the only way to get to heaven is through faith in Christ—but I still think I'm a pretty good person, and I can't see why God would condemn me just because I've never accepted Christ as my Savior."

Whatever God has told you to do, you'd better do it. Otherwise you are fighting against God, as surely as these armies of the earth that will gather in the Middle East.

I'm not saying you will lose your salvation if you don't give to God's work or attend church on Sunday. But if you know what God expects of you and you refuse to do it, then He is not truly the Lord of your life, and your confession of Christ's Lordship is vain. You might be among those of whom Jesus spoke when He said, "Not everyone who says to me, 'Lord, Lord,' will enter the kingdom of heaven, but only he who does the will of my Father who is in heaven" (Matthew 7:21).

There are others who fight against God in a more active manner and know exactly what they're doing. These are the humanists who want to exclude God from every facet of our society. They don't want God to be mentioned, so they protest Christmas pageants staged by schoolchildren. They exclude mention of God in school textbooks, even though belief in Him has been a major shaping force in our nation's history. They produce TV shows and movies that ridicule Him and those who believe in Him.

So far, God seems to be remarkably patient with such people. But as we've already seen, His patience will not last forever.

And I certainly wouldn't want to be in the position of having to face Him when it runs out.

The Beast Is Captured

> Then I saw the beast and the kings of the earth and their armies gathered together to make war against the rider on the horse and his army. But the beast was captured, and with him the false prophet who had performed the miraculous signs on his behalf. With these signs he had deluded those who had received the mark of the beast and worshiped his image. The two of them were thrown alive into the fiery lake of burning sulfur.   Revelation 19:19–20

It's almost anticlimactic, isn't it? All the armies of the earth will be gathered together. We would expect a battle of immense proportions to take place—but it won't. Instead, Jesus will reach out and capture the Beast and his top general without the least bit of trouble.

While the world has stood in awe of the power of the Antichrist and questioned who could possibly make war with him, Paul tells us in 2 Thessalonians 2:8 that "the Lord shall consume [him] with the spirit of his mouth, and shall destroy [him] with the brightness of his coming" (KJV).

How we fail to comprehend the tremendous power of the Word of the Lord!

The Scripture tells us that the two of them will be cast into the lake of fire, which in Greek is called *Gehenna.* This will be the final home for the unrighteous dead, the place God prepared for Satan and his angels. The Beast and his false prophet will be the first to be imprisoned here.

What sort of place will it be? Jesus describes it as a place of utter darkness, where there will be weeping and gnashing of teeth. (See Matthew 25:30 and Luke 13:22–28.)

This is how Christ will deal with the Antichrist, but what about all the armies gathered in support of him?

John tells us that they "were killed with the sword that came out of the mouth of the rider on the horse, and all the birds gorged themselves on their flesh" (verse 21).

What sword will come out of the mouth of Jesus and destroy His enemies? His Word.

Genesis tells us how God spoke the universe into existence. He said, "Let there be light," and there *was* light. Everything came into existence through the words that came out of His mouth. All Christ, the Word of God, has to do is speak the word and His enemies will be utterly destroyed.

The armies of the world will think their firepower is a match for God Himself, but instead they'll find destruction coming upon them in a matter of moments, just as mighty Babylon will be destroyed in a single hour.

And now the Middle Eastern countryside will be covered with the corpses of those who dared to fight against God. Everywhere bodies will rot in the sun.

It won't be a pleasant picture, but it will be a fitting end to those who dare to raise their fists in defiance of God Himself.

A Thousand Years of Peace

Once the final "battle," which was not really much of a battle at all, has been completed, John says:

> And I saw an angel coming down out of heaven, having the key to the Abyss and holding in his hand a great chain. He seized the dragon, that ancient serpent, who is the devil, or Satan, and bound him for a thousand years. He threw him into the Abyss, and locked and sealed it over

him, to keep him from deceiving the nations any more
until the thousand years were ended. After that, he must
be set free for a short time.		Revelation 20:1–3

You may remember that when we talked about the fifth
trumpet sounding to bring forth one of God's judgments, there
was an angel who unlocked the door to the Abyss (or the
bottomless pit), and thus set free a horde of demonic creatures
to wreak havoc upon the earth.

Now another angel will come to reverse the process. The
demons will have done everything within their power to destroy
the plans of God, but will have succeeded only in helping to
fulfill it.

It's interesting to notice how many times God takes Satan's
worst attempts to harm us and turns them to our benefit. How
Satan and his demons must have rejoiced when they saw Christ
nailed to the cross, thinking they had succeeded in killing Him
and thereby thwarting God's plan to save mankind! Surely it
was an army of demons that whispered into the ears of the
crowd as Jesus was on trial and caused them to cry out, "Crucify Him! Crucify Him!" But Satan didn't realize the death of
Christ was no defeat at all. It was God's greatest victory, providing all mankind with a way of escape from their sins.

I think, too, of the story of Joseph. Remember how his
brothers sold him into slavery because they hated him, but God
used their evil deed to exalt Joseph to a position of prominence
in Egypt? When his brothers were afraid he would harm them
because of what they had done, he told them, "You intended
to harm me, but God intended it for good to accomplish what
is now being done, the saving of many lives" (Genesis 50:20).

That's the way it is with God. Life is not filled with calm seas
and blue skies. Things happen that cause pain and trouble. But
if we are trusting in God, He will take the worst events and use
them for our benefit.

As it says in Romans 8:28, "And we know that in all things

God works for the good of those who love him, who have been called according to his purpose."

Once again, Satan's worst intentions will have, in effect, played right into God's hands. He will have been revealed as nothing more than a second-rate power, helpless when confronted with the power of God. The Antichrist who sought to deceive the nations has himself been deceived. He thought he was getting away with thumbing his nose at God because God was powerless to stop him. But only God's patience and permission enabled him to get away with anything.

I am reminded, once again, of how I often feel when I see the news on TV or read my morning newspaper. A man is charged with killing his tiny son. A group of teenagers shoot and kill a convenience store clerk "just for the fun of it." A man who has made millions of dollars selling illegal drugs has thwarted the law once again, his case thrown out of court on a technicality.

Sometimes I am tempted to ask, "How long will God stand back and let people get away with these things? Doesn't He care?"

Yes, He does care. And these criminals who think they are above the law, God's or man's, aren't getting away with anything at all. God will finally pronounce judgment against them, just as He will with the Antichrist and his followers.

And now, John says:

> I saw thrones on which were seated those who had been given authority to judge. And I saw the souls of those who had been beheaded because of their testimony for Jesus and because of the word of God. They had not worshiped the beast or his image and had not received his mark on their foreheads or their hands. They came to life and reigned with Christ a thousand years. (The rest of the dead did not come to life until the thousand years were ended.) This is the first resurrection. Blessed and holy are those who have part in the first resurrection. The second death

has no power over them, but they will be priests of God
and of Christ and will reign with him for a thousand years.
                                        Revelation 20:4–6

After the violence and turmoil of the past several thousand
years—especially of the last seven years—peace will settle over
the planet. Jesus Christ will leave His throne in heaven and be
enthroned in His chosen capital, His beloved Jerusalem.

This city that rejected Him so cruelly during His previous
earthly ministry will welcome Him with open arms. No longer
will the cries ring out, "Crucify Him! Crucify Him!" Instead,
it will be as the prophet Zechariah foretold: "They will look on
me, the one they have pierced, and they will mourn for him as
one mourns for an only child, and grieve bitterly for him as one
grieves for a firstborn son" (Zechariah 12:10).

Now it will be obvious that He is the Messiah, and the Jews
in Jerusalem will weep because they rejected that truth for so
many years.

They resisted the Antichrist, not because they believed in
Jesus, but because of the blasphemies he committed when he
moved into God's Temple and declared himself to be God. But
as Jesus returns to His holy city, they will fall to their knees and
acknowledge Him as Lord and Savior. The Millennium has
arrived.

As Jesus takes up residence in His world capital, other members of His Church will take their places besides Him. These are
the righteous who served the Lord, even until death, and now
they will reign with Him forever. The twelve apostles will undoubtedly be given positions of great authority, but so will
many Christians whose names are little-known. People who
served God steadfastly during times of trial will now be re-
warded. Perhaps *you* will be made a president, a governor, or
a mayor. There are thousands of positions of leadership
throughout the world, and all of these will go to people who
have proved their loyalty to Christ.

This thousand-year period will be the best the earth has ever known. There will be no war. Crime will be nonexistent. Satan will be locked up where he can't cause any trouble. People will live with an eternal perspective and won't be so driven by ambition and selfishness. The fear of death will not hang over everyone, because God Himself, in the Person of Jesus Christ, sits on the throne.

Have you ever heard someone say, "I could believe in God if only He would give me a sign—if only He would speak to me in an audible voice or reveal Himself to me"?

Well, during the thousand-year reign of Christ, there won't be any reason at all to doubt, because Christ will be upon the earth in a physical way. He will preside over world affairs, and everyone will be able to see Him.

Have you ever heard anyone say, "I'd like to believe in George Bush, but I just need more proof that he exists"?

If you have, then you've been talking to a pretty strange character. I don't think there's any doubt that George Bush is real, and that he was elected as President of the United States. During the reign of Christ, no one will doubt that He is the Son of God. Can you imagine what a glorious time this is going to be?

And yet not everyone will be happy. Some will begin to resist the rule of Christ, especially as time goes by. Children will be born into the world, and some of them will grow up never knowing anything but Christ's government. They won't remember the violence and destruction, and how it was when man was free to let his worst passions reign unchecked. They will begin to chafe under Christ's rule, and wish that someone a bit more "progressive" would take over.

After all, Christ is not going to be the most easygoing, "look-the-other-way" sort of king. He will be fair, but He is going to demand righteousness. Perhaps we have the idea that because this is the Millennium and because Satan is locked up, everyone on the planet will be righteous. But this will still be earth, not heaven, and man's nature will still be man's nature.

Human beings don't need Satan to tempt us to evil. We have enough evil in our own hearts, and I sometimes think Satan gets the blame for a lot of things he has absolutely nothing to do with.

Even under Christ's rule, men will be tempted to cheat, steal, lie, and seduce their neighbors' wives. The problem is that nothing—absolutely nothing—will escape detection and judgment.

I can hear the anger and frustration now: "For crying out loud, all I did was break one little rule. Can't you give me a break?"

Jesus' judgments will be tempered with mercy, but that won't be enough for some people.

Please understand that most of the people on the planet will be radiantly happy. But some will come to hate Christ and everything He stands for. In essence, they will begin to long for the return of Satan. And they're going to get what they want.

Satan's Last Gasp

When the thousand years are over, Satan will be released from his prison and will go out to deceive the nations in the four corners of the earth—God and Magog—to gather them for battle. In number they are like the sand on the seashore. They marched across the breadth of the earth and surrounded the camp of God's people, the city he loves.

Revelation 20:7–9

For a thousand years, Satan will have been locked away deep in the bowels of the earth. Surely this time of peace and serenity will go on forever . . . won't it?

No, just when it seemed safe to live on planet earth . . . all of a sudden Satan will be back. And we can be sure that a thousand years locked in the pit won't have made his personality the least bit sweeter.

Now Satan won't get out of the pit by tunneling his way through the earth. The Bible says he will be "set free," and that means God will have allowed it to happen. Satan's pride will have blinded him to the point where he will still believe he can overthrow God. What he won't realize is that he is now going about the business of fulfilling God's final plans for this planet.

It's amazing, too, but true, that there will still be thousands, perhaps even millions of people on this planet who will choose to believe Satan's deceptions.

Some people believe that the passage about Gog and Magog (verse 8) speaks of the same events of Ezekiel 38. The events of Ezekiel 38 and Revelation 20 are separated by at least 1,000 years. In Ezekiel 38 Gog the chief prince of Magog comes against the newly formed nation of Israel. Here Gog and Magog come against the reign of Christ. The results are the same, with God's fire destroying them.

The Bible is not clear as to how this will happen. It's beyond my understanding that anyone would want to trade God's love for the lies and hatred of the devil. But God says that's exactly what's going to happen, and I have no choice but to believe Him.

Now once again, the holy city of Jerusalem will find itself under siege. Satan's armies will have surrounded God's chosen city, and it appears as though victory will be in the devil's grasp.

But sudden destruction will rain down. Verse 9:

. . . Fire came down from heaven and devoured them.

The rebellion will be over, almost before it begins. And John says,

> And the devil, who deceived them, was thrown into the
> lake of burning sulfur, where the beast and the false
> prophet had been thrown. They will be tormented day and
> night for ever and ever.   Revelation 20:10

It will finally be over. Evil will have suffered its ultimate
defeat. The universe will have been cleansed.

Men will never again have to wrestle with the origin of evil
and wonder how it could exist in God's universe. The universe
will have been set free, and the world as we know it will have
melted away.

What has happened to the earth? Remember how fire came
out of heaven to destroy Satan and all his armies? The Bible
does not say for certain, but it could be that this was a nuclear
explosion that set off a chain reaction, resulting in the destruction of the entire planet. It could be that Satan's own efforts to
capture the planet backfired in his face. It wouldn't be the first
time.

Whatever has happened, the earth no longer exists.

The apostle Peter prophesied that this day would come, and
he saw it this way:

> . . . The day of the Lord will come like a thief. The heavens
> will disappear with a roar; the elements will be destroyed
> by fire, and the earth and everything in it will be laid bare.
>   2 Peter 3:10

Actually, a better translation is that "the earth and everything in it will be burned up."

Whatever has happened, the earth has passed from the scene.
Time is finished and eternity has begun. Judgment Day has
come at last.

11

A World Reborn

Revelation 20:11–22:21

Then I saw a great white throne and him who was seated
on it. Earth and sky fled from his presence, and there was
no place for them.

And I saw the dead, great and small, standing before the
throne, and books were opened. Another book was
opened, which is the book of life. The dead were judged
according to what they had done as recorded in the books.
The sea gave up the dead that were in it, and death and
Hades gave up the dead that were in them, and each
person was judged according to what he had done.

Revelation 20:11–13

Judgment Day will have arrived, a day of unspeakable horror
for those newly resurrected people who will stand before God's
Great White Throne. Horror, because they are about to be
condemned for all eternity, and they know it. They may stam-
mer and stutter, but they will have no defense for themselves,
and no reason why they neglected to accept the free gift of
salvation offered them by Jesus Christ.

There will already have been one resurrection, that of the
righteous dead who have risen to live and reign with Christ
during His millennial reign on earth. And now the unrighteous
dead will stand before the throne.

We've all seen the cartoons of St. Peter sitting at the Pearly

Gates holding a big book. As newly arrived people come up to him, he takes a look in the book to see if they have a "reservation," much the way the maître d' at a restaurant would do.

Well, that scene won't really happen, but that big book actually exists and it's called the Book of Life. If you belong to Jesus Christ, your name is written in the Book. If you don't, it isn't.

John says that people are going to be judged according to what they have done. But we know that everyone who has ever lived has sinned, and nobody tainted by sin is going to be allowed into heaven. Furthermore, there is only one way to be cleansed of sin—by accepting Christ as our personal Savior.

Those who have accepted Christ, therefore, and done their best to live for Him have their names written in the Book of Life. Those who have never turned their lives over to Christ are not listed in it.

It's thrilling to me to think that there is an actual Book sitting in heaven that has my name in it. God can flip over to "S" and look until he comes across the name *Smith*. He can look down the list of Smiths and there it will be, *Chuck Smith*. If you are a Christian, your name is in that book, too.

Don't misunderstand. God knows each and every one of us personally. He doesn't need a book to tell Him who's going to get into heaven and who isn't. But He has one just the same.

You know as well as I do that there are a lot of charlatans out there making a good living from "Christianity." I put the word in quotes because it's not true Christianity, but a strange mixture of Christ and superstition. They sell their "miracle crosses," raising millions of dollars by preying on the superstitions and fears of gullible people. This is another instance about which I want to ask, How long will God stand back and permit this to happen? But there is a day of reckoning coming.

Can you imagine how terrified these hucksters are going to be when Judgment Day arrives? All those years they thought they were playing empty games to make a few dollars, and now they find out that they were making light of the Son of God.

"I didn't mean anything by it. I didn't know You were real, Lord!"

But He is real, and He tells them to depart from Him because He never knew them.

How terribly sad to be so close to the truth without recognizing it!

One by one they will be judged and thrown into the awful lake of fire.

> Then death and Hades were thrown into the lake of fire. The lake of fire is the second death. If anyone's name was not found written in the book of life, he was thrown into the lake of fire.   Revelation 20:14–15

Evil cannot be ignored. It has to be destroyed once and for all. God is patient, kind, loving, not willing that any should perish. But despite His best efforts to reach all men, many have still turned away from Him. It is not His hand that will send them into the fire—rather, their own misdeeds.

> . . . The cowardly, the unbelieving, the vile, the murderers, the sexually immoral, those who practice magic arts, the idolaters and all liars—their place will be in the fiery lake of burning sulfur. This is the second death.
>
> Revelation 21:8

But this is not a time to dwell on terror. It is a time of bright new beginnings.

> Then I saw a new heaven and a new earth, for the first heaven and the first earth had passed away, and there was no longer any sea. I saw the Holy City, the new Jerusalem, coming down out of heaven from God, prepared as a bride beautifully dressed for her husband. And I heard a loud voice from the throne saying, "Now the dwelling of

God is with men, and he will live with them. They will
be his people, and God himself will be with them and
be their God. He will wipe every tear from their eyes.
There will be no more death or mourning or crying or
pain, for the old order of things has passed away."

Revelation 21:1–4

It will be like the dawning of a beautiful new day after a
heavy rain has cleansed the atmosphere.

If you've ever spent any time in Los Angeles, you know how
smoggy it can get, especially in the summer when a heat wave
comes to town, and the smog just seems to lie there like a thick,
choking blanket.

How good it is when a rainy day comes and washes it all
away! After the rain has stopped, the sky is clear and blue.
Everything smells so good. The San Gabriel Mountains—
which you couldn't even see because of the smog a couple of
days back—look close enough to touch. It can make you almost
giddy.

That's what it's going to be like when God creates a new
heaven and a new earth. Everything bad that was connected to
the old earth will be gone forever. All the beauty that we found
on this earth will be magnified many times over. Pain will be
gone. Death will be gone. Evil will be gone.

Those who were blind will have better than 20/20 vision.
Those who were deaf will hear all the beautiful sounds of God's
new creation. Those who were crippled will run and jump and
feel so strong they can't keep still. Those who couldn't speak
will shout out their praises to God. All that was bad will disappear, and all that's left will be beauty and joy—to last forever!

And the City of New Jerusalem itself is going to be dazzling
in its beauty.

John is taken by an angel to the top of a great mountain,
where he sees the Holy City coming down out of heaven. He
says,

> It shone with the glory of God, and its brilliance was like
> that of a very precious jewel, like a jasper, clear as crystal.
>
> Revelation 21:11

As the angel goes on to measure the City the apostle watches, taking in the breathtaking sights—the streets of gold, gates of pearl, and precious stones everywhere.

The angel who measures it reports that it is a perfect cube, measuring roughly 1,400 miles in all directions.

This makes it just a tiny bit smaller than the moon, and I believe this City will actually be in orbit around the new earth.

This will be a city of incredible size. Some quick arithmetic reveals that it will contain 980 million cubic miles. I can't explain how a city could be a cube, but I believe we will not be captive to our old perceptions of space or time. We will perhaps be *dimensional,* able to live within as well as upon. It is interesting that most of the planets and observable stellar objects appear in the shape of a ball, while this new heavenly object will be in the form of a cube. In any case, we will have a totally new way of looking at God's creation, perhaps in four or five dimensions.

The New Jerusalem is not going to be a city like New York, where people live in skyscraper apartment buildings, jammed one on top of the other. There will be more people there than any city that exists currently upon the earth, but there will be plenty of room just the same.

There will be no crowding, no clutter, no smog, none of the problems associated with today's biggest cities. But best of all, there will be none of the physical, emotional, or spiritual problems that so often handicap us today. There will be no physical infirmities, no weaknesses, no weariness, no sorrow of any kind. It sounds almost too good to be true, doesn't it?

No wonder the angel tells John, in verse five of chapter 21, "Write this down, for these words are trustworthy and true."

It's as if the angel is saying, "I know this is so wonderful that it's almost beyond belief, but I guarantee you that every word is true."

There is another promise from Jesus in verses six and seven:

> "It is done. I am the Alpha and the Omega, the Beginning and the End. To him who is thirsty I will give to drink without cost from the spring of the water of life. He who overcomes will inherit all this, and I will be his God and he will be my son."

You may remember the conversation our Lord had with the woman at the well as recorded in John 4. He told her, "If you knew the gift of God and who it is that asks you for a drink, you would have asked him and he would have given you living water" (verse 10).

The woman didn't understand what He was talking about, especially since He had no bucket with which to draw water from the well. But then Jesus explained that "everyone who drinks this water will be thirsty again, but whoever drinks the water I give him will never thirst. Indeed, the water I give him will become in him a spring of water welling up to eternal life" (verses 13–14).

How true this is!

I remember talking to a young woman who had spent several years of her life pursuing fulfillment through religious experience. She had tried every form of Eastern religion, she'd been a member of a New Age cult, she'd investigated the occult. She would stay for a little while with one group, then grow disillusioned and flit on over to another group. Nowhere did she find peace of mind. Then she met Jesus.

That was the day her search ended.

"The day I accepted Christ as my Lord and Savior," she said, "something happened inside of me. Immediately I knew I had found all the peace and contentment I had been looking for all those years. I found something else, too—a reason for living."

Jesus gives the water of the Spirit to us today. But in the New Jerusalem we will be able to drink of it in a new, much stronger way. The days of peaks and valleys will be over and we will live each moment surrounded by joy.

Living in God's Presence

Have you ever been in a situation in which you felt the presence of God very strongly? Perhaps you were praying alone in your bedroom, and suddenly you just knew God was there. His presence was almost palpable, and you felt you could reach out and touch His face. Or it could have been in a church service when the entire congregation was singing a hymn of praise. Maybe it was when someone else was praying for you and you began to sense His presence in that prayer. Perhaps your heart began to beat a little faster, and you felt lightheaded and a little weak in the knees in His presence. But most of all you felt a great, great joy and happiness.

Most of us have had experiences like those. So imagine how wonderful it will be for us in the New Jerusalem when we live in God's presence at all times. I don't know about you, but it's hard for me to wait!

We know that this Holy City will shine with the glory of God, and that its brilliance will be like that of a jasper, which is an opaque, often highly colored quartz. What else do we know?

> It had a great, high wall with twelve gates, and with twelve angels at the gates. On the gates were written the names of the twelve tribes of Israel. There were three gates on the east, three on the north, three on the south and three on the west. The wall of the city had twelve foundations, and on them were the names of the twelve apostles of the Lamb.   Revelation 21:12–14

The fact that the names of the twelve tribes of Israel will be written on the gates points up that those righteous men and women from Old Testament days will be residing within this City of God, while the names of the twelve apostles represent those of us who have served God through the Church of Jesus Christ. Abraham will be here. So will Elijah and Moses. The apostle Paul also will be here, as will the great men and women of faith of our own day.

Can you imagine sitting at the feet of Noah and listening as he tells the story of the Great Flood? Or listening to Moses as he tells about his encounter with the evil Pharaoh?

We already talked about the Tower of Babel, where God supernaturally gave men different languages. In the New Jerusalem, all those cultural differences will disappear. There will be no more races, colors, or language differences; we will all exist in perfect unity.

As the angel to whom John has been talking goes to measure the City with "a measuring rod of gold," the apostle describes some of the other elements of the city.

> The wall was made of jasper, and the city of pure gold, as pure as glass. The foundations of the city walls were decorated with every kind of precious stone. The first foundation was jasper, the second sapphire, the third chalcedony, the fourth emerald, the fifth sardonyx, the sixth carnelian, the seventh chrysolite, the eighth beryl, the ninth topaz, the tenth chrysoprase, the eleventh jacinth, and the twelfth amethyst.   Revelation 21:18–20

We don't know for certain the identities of all these stones, but we know that they are beautiful and precious. No wonder John describes the City descending from heaven as "a glorious sight, beautiful as a bride at her wedding" (TLB).

It will be sparkling with a dazzling array of colors as it descends from heaven.

If we turn to Exodus 28:15–21, we see that the Old Testament priests often wore breastplates containing the same precious stones as those that decorate the foundations of the Holy City. When the priests wore those breastplates they were, in effect, looking forward to New Jerusalem and the eternal salvation God would provide through His Son.

John goes on to explain that the twelve gates into the City consist of twelve pearls, and that each gate is made of a single pearl. As for the main street of the City, it is made of pure gold, "like transparent glass" (verse 21).

God's Values vs. Man's Values

Why will the Holy City be full of precious metals and stones?

I believe it's because God knows that mortal men have often shipwrecked their souls in the pursuit of such wealth. Instead of seeking after the Word of God, which lasts forever, they've chased after gold or diamonds. They've cheated, robbed, even killed to get this sort of wealth, which never benefits them more than a few years. A man may spend his entire life in pursuit of material wealth, but in the end his fate is the same as that of any other man: He dies and leaves it all behind.

How tragic if his pursuit of earthly gain has kept him out of the Kingdom of God!

God shows us now that our earthly value system is totally out of kilter. All these things for which men will lie, kill, and steal have absolutely no value in heaven. There, gold is so plentiful they use it instead of asphalt or concrete! Jewels are beautiful, yes, and a delight to the senses, but they are not of lasting importance.

In Revelation 21:22–27, John has some beautiful words about the conditions of life in the City:

> I did not see a temple in the city, because the Lord God
> Almighty and the Lamb are its temple. The city does not
> need the sun or the moon to shine on it, for the glory of
> God gives it light, and the Lamb is its lamp. The nations
> will walk by its light, and the kings of the earth will bring
> their splendor into it. On no day will its gates ever be shut,
> for there will be no night there. The glory and honor of
> the nations will be brought into it. Nothing impure will
> ever enter it, nor will anyone who does what is shameful
> or deceitful, but only those whose names are written in the
> Lamb's book of life.

We can see from this that the access into New Jerusalem will
be limited, but apparently there will be some coming and going.

John has already told us that there will be a new earth, so
it is quite possible that God will have created a new order upon
the earth. He doesn't tell us, but there is no reason we should
try to limit Him.

Many mysteries of God have not yet been revealed to us. He
has given us everything we need to obtain eternal life, but there
are many secrets that are yet to be uncovered. I'm looking
forward to a glorious time in eternity uncovering the mysteries
of God!

And now John sees

> the river of the water of life, as clear as crystal, flowing
> from the throne of God and of the Lamb down the middle
> of the great street of the city.   Revelation 22:1–2

There are trees here, too, but not ordinary trees.

> On each side of the river stood the tree of life, bearing
> twelve crops of fruit, yielding its fruit every month. And
> the leaves of the tree are for the healing of the nations. No
> longer will there be any curse.   Revelation 22:2–3

I am reminded of a tree that grew in our yard when I was a boy. This tree had various types of citrus fruits grafted together. It bore both navel and Valencia oranges, as well as grapefruit and lemons. During part of the year we could pick Valencia oranges, during the winter months navel oranges; and in the meantime we could eat grapefruit for breakfast and drink lemonade with dinner.

Nowadays you can buy trees that have peaches and nectarines growing together. Scientists are doing many interesting and different things with fruit trees.

But in the City of New Jerusalem this tree yields a different type of fruit every month! I love fruit, and think I'll try to get a few similar trees planted in my yard when I get to the Holy City!

The Curse Is Removed

If we go back and read the account of Adam and Eve's fall from God's grace, we find these words that God spoke to Adam: "Cursed is the ground because of you; through painful toil you will eat of it all the days of your life. It will produce thorns and thistles for you, and you will eat the plants of the field. By the sweat of your brow you will eat your food . . ." (Genesis 3:17–19).

But now there is no more curse. Instead of bringing forth thorns and thistles, the soil in New Jerusalem brings forth trees that bear fruit every month, and whose leaves "are for the healing of the nations."

We know there will be no sickness within the Holy City, so it would make sense that there will be a new order existing on the earth itself. The leaves of these trees will be used to cure whatever sicknesses exist among these people.

That there will be a new generation of men upon the earth also makes sense in light of John's comment in Revelation 22:5

that residents of the Holy City will "reign for ever and ever."
How can a king reign unless there are subjects for him to rule?
Apparently the residents of New Jerusalem will rule over those
who live upon the new earth God has created.

What else can we say about living conditions in New Jerusalem? We will be able to look into the face of God Himself! There
will be no night at all but continuous, glorious day! Again, it
almost sounds too good to be true. That's why the angel is so
quick to say, "These words are trustworthy and true" (verse 6).

And now, as we come to the last fifteen verses of the last book
of the Bible, Jesus Himself speaks:

> "Behold, I am coming soon! Blessed is he who keeps the
> words of the prophecy in this book."   Revelation 22:7

Then the angel who has been showing John all the joys of
New Jerusalem tells him not to seal up the words of the prophecy of this book,

> ". . . because the time is near. Let him who does wrong
> continue to do wrong; let him who is vile continue to be
> vile; let him who does right continue to do right; and let
> him who is holy continue to be holy."
>   Revelation 22:10–11

When Daniel had a vision of the events of the end times, by
contrast, the angel told him "the words are closed up and sealed
until the time of the end" (Daniel 12:9).

In other words, Daniel had been given the prophecy, and he
did not fully understand it. This was all right, though, because
it was not yet time for a complete understanding to be revealed.

Now the angel gives John the opposite message. These words
are *not* to be sealed. They are for all men and women to hear
because Jesus is coming quickly, and all these things will come
to pass.

"Behold, I am coming soon! My reward is with me, and I will give to everyone according to what he has done. I am the Alpha and the Omega, the First and the Last, the Beginning and the End.

"Blessed are those who wash their robes, that they may have the right to the tree of life and may go through the gates into the city. Outside are the dogs, those who practice magic arts, the sexually immoral, the murderers, the idolaters and everyone who loves and practices falsehood.

"I, Jesus, have sent my angel to give you this testimony for the churches. I am the Root and the Offspring of David, and the bright Morning Star."

Revelation 22:12–16

Note that when Jesus says He sent His angel to give "you" this testimony, He is not speaking to John alone. The Greek word used here is plural. *You* refers to everyone who hears this prophecy, including you and me!

And so we come to the final few verses of this marvelous book. In verse 17 John says that any who are thirsty may come to Christ and receive the free gift of the water of life.

Jesus will not refuse any who come to Him. If you will, through faith, accept Him as your Lord and Savior, you will be saved. If you understand that He died in your behalf, to cleanse you of your sins, you may accept His sacrifice and stand righteous before God.

That, above everything else, is what the book of Revelation is about.

This world is already divided into two camps—those who belong to God and those who don't. Trouble and persecution are coming, and there's nothing we can do to alter that fact. This is the holy and perfect plan of God for this fallen world.

Those who don't belong to God face an eternity of utter, stark horror. But for those who belong to God through faith in Christ, the troubles planet earth is about to experience will vanish quickly into an eternity of glorious beauty, peace, and joy.

Above all of the prophecies recorded in this book, this is the matter of utmost importance. The question is, Whose side are *you* on?

The book closes with a warning—and a blessing.

In Revelation 22:18–21 we read:

> I warn everyone who hears the words of the prophecy of this book: If anyone adds anything to them, God will add to him the plagues described in this book. And if anyone takes words away from this book of prophecy, God will take away from him his share in the tree of life and in the holy city, which are described in this book.
>
> He who testifies to these things says, "Yes, I am coming soon."
>
> Amen. Come, Lord Jesus.
>
> The grace of the Lord Jesus be with God's people. Amen.

Amen and amen!